The New Economics of Richard Nixon:
Freezes, Floats, and Fiscal Policy

The New Economics
of Richard Nixon

Freezes, Floats, and Fiscal Policy

ROGER LEROY MILLER
University of Washington
and
National Economic Research Associates

RABURN M. WILLIAMS
University of Hawaii

Canfield Press, San Francisco
A Department of Harper & Row, Publishers, Inc.
New York/Evanston/San Francisco/London

THE NEW ECONOMICS OF RICHARD NIXON:
FREEZES, FLOATS, AND FISCAL POLICY

Standard Book Number: 06-385448-1

Library of Congress Catalog Card Number: 77-184417

72 73 74 75 9 8 7 6 5 4 3 2 1

Preface

When President Nixon and his economic advisors were dining after their grueling NEP* weekend at Camp David in August 1971, one of them said, "Everyone here should get a Ph.D. in economics."

Seven weeks later a relaxed and contented Richard Nixon (Ph.D.?) was able to report "that the wage-price freeze has been remarkably successful," that "our campaign to create a new monetary stability and bring a new fairness to world trade" has been successful, and finally "that the House of Representatives yesterday [October 6, 1971] passed a tax program based on my recommendations that will create an additional half million new jobs in the coming year."

The President knew he had a good thing going, so he set up a Price Commission and a Pay Board. He said he didn't want a bureaucracy but, nonetheless, kept the Cost of Living Council extant in order to "back up the Pay Board and the Price Commission with government sanctions where necessary."

In order to catch hold of all loose ends, Nixon also appointed a government committee on interest and dividends headed by his old friend Dr. Arthur Burns, chairman of the Board of Governors of the Federal Reserve System.

So now we have it: The NEP dreamed up and implemented by a man whose 1968 political platform was built on

*New Economic Program

government non-intervention and individual enterprise. Who could have imagined that on October 7, 1971, Richard Milhous Nixon would be telling us, "What is best for all of us is best for each of us"? The Adam Smiths of the world must have turned over twice in their graves on that day.

We felt compelled to write this book about the NEP because so little analysis of the *real* economic content of Nixon's programs has been presented. We think readers will end up realizing that there is more politics in R.M. Nixon's economics than there is anything else.

For example, any freeze on dividends will do nothing because corporations will merely invest their extra profits and stockholders will get capital gains instead of more dividends.

For example, Nixon's refusal to convert dollars into gold has been economic reality since 1968, when we went on a two-tier gold price system.

And, while we feel that Nixon's fiscal policies will funnel demand into sectors with excess capacity—autos, machine tools, and computers—there was no overall *net* stimulus to the economy implicit in his NEP. His promised creation of 500,000 new jobs by mere congressional enactment of his tax package seems exaggerated, to say the least. Careful economic analysis tells a different story. In the following pages we present this analysis and more. We explain why wage and price controls are useless at best and destructive at worst. To allow readers the opportunity to get the full flavor of Nixon's New Economics, we have provided an appendix with his NEP speech, his price freeze Executive Order, and other related materials.

We wish to thank Susan Vita Miller for helping to rework the manuscript and Judith Ann Williams for her similar heroic efforts. William Burgower pushed us into this project and for that we are appreciative.

The views expressed herein are those of the authors and are not necessarily those of the institutions with which they are affiliated.

R. L. M., Seattle
R. M. W., Honolulu
November 1971

Contents

Preface   v

1. The "New" Game Plan   1

2. The Path to an Inflationary Recession   4

3. A Little History of Controlled Prices   10

4. Nixon's 90-Day Freeze,
   or How to Stump the Democrats   17

5. Tax Credits and Job Development   25

6. "I Am Now a Keynesian"—Richard Nixon, 1971   31

7. The Fed's Fascination with Interest Rates   36

8. The Fall of Fixed Exchange Rates   45

9. Floats and Fables of Gold   54

10. Tariffs Bring Joy to the Hearts of Many
    (GM, U.S. Steel, and Motorola)   62

11. What's So New?   67

    Appendix A: Remarks of the President on Nation-
    wide Radio and Television, August 15, 1971   70

    Appendix B: Economic Stabilization Act of 1970
    (As Amended)   77

    Appendix C: Executive Order Providing for Stabili-
    zation of Prices, Rents, Wages, and Salaries   79

    Appendix D: Imposition of Supplemental Duty for
    Balance of Payments Purposes   83

    Index   87

The "New" Game Plan 1

At 8:15 P.M., EDT, August 15, 1971, in the East Room of the White House, the Honorable John M. Connally, Secretary of the Treasury, held a press conference. The members of the press were told that the TV would soon be turned on so that a turned off nation could see President Nixon present one of the most dramatic political speeches on economic policy since FDR's in 1933. Secretary Connally told the press that the speech would reflect decisions taken because the nation had "an unacceptable level of unemployment, an unacceptable rate of inflation, and the need for a continuing and expanding economy [sic], a deteriorating balance of trade, a very unsatisfactory balance of payments situation, plus a continuing uncertainty and instability in the international monetary markets."

Nixon's speech was everything promised and even more. He proposed the following:

1. a freeze on wages, prices, and rents for 90 days
2. tax cuts totaling $6.3 billion in the current fiscal year—specifically:

   a. a repeal of the 7 percent excise tax on automobiles

   b. acceleration to January 1, 1972, of a $50 increase in personal income tax exemptions and an increase in the minimum standard deduction to 15 percent or a maximum of $2,000, both originally scheduled to occur the following year

   c. a 10 percent investment tax credit on new, U.S.-built capital equipment retroactive to August 15, dropping to 5 percent on August 15, 1972

3. a 10 percent surcharge on all dutiable imports

4. government spending cuts of $4.7 billion, resulting primarily from the temporary deferral of the revenue-sharing and welfare reform programs then before Congress and a 6-month freeze on a government pay increase planned for January 1

In addition Nixon announced that the United States would no longer sell gold to foreign central banks at $35 an ounce, thusly putting the world officially on a "dollar standard."[1]

Many Republicans and even some Democrats voted for Richard Nixon in 1968 because he was a firm believer in a minimum of government intervention. During his first years as President he did, in fact, opt for a reduction in federal economic "tinkering." But just as those who voted for Johnson because he was the peace candidate found themselves as involved with Vietnam as we were to become, so those who voted for Nixon because he was a free market advocate found themselves saddled with a wage and price freeze, the legal basis of which was the Economic Stabilization Act of 1970.[2] No one reading the Executive Order Providing for Stabilization of Prices, Rents, Wages, and Salaries[3] would even have suspected that a Republican President could sign it.

An ex-plumber named George Meany, president of the nation's largest union organization, called the wage and price freeze a "Robin Hood in reverse—robbing the poor to pay the rich." Meany's bitterness seemed to have emanated from a

---

[1] The complete text of President Nixon's speech is given in Appendix A.
[2] See Appendix B for complete text.
[3] See Appendix C for complete text.

firm conviction that the President's economic program was weighted in favor of big business and against labor. Nixon had not included any limit on the amount of profits and interest or divided income that could be accumulated during the 90-day freeze period. Labor Secretary James B. Hodgson indicated that he was "saddened" by Meany's public distaste for the new economics of Richard Nixon. Hodgson said further, "Mr. Meany appears to be sadly out of step with the needs and desires of America's working men and women."

After the announcement of the new economic policy, the Democrats quickly attempted to recapture some of the clothes that had been stolen from them while they were out swimming. Democratic presidential hopefuls remained stunned for some time but eventually came up with "appropriate" criticisms. Democratic congressmen such as Representative Al Ullman sat back and said "I can just sit back and say I told you so": he had been urging wage and price controls for at least two and a half years. It was a certainty that both the Democratic-ruled House and the Senate would play politics with the administration's proposals as soon as Congress reconvened. One member of the influential House Rules Committee said, "You can be assured the program will not leave the House in the same form as it arrived. Once the President has opened the door we [Democrats] will try to pry it open further."

Before attempting to assess what Nixon's new economics is all about, we first should figure out how the country got into the economic mess that presumably forced such momentous decisions on the administration. And we should realize that the ups and downs leading to this mess were somewhat out of the ordinary in the annals of U.S. economic history. The sixties represented perhaps the largest sustained period of an ever-increasing standard of living that Americans have experienced. Moreover, the period of rising prices in 1965 represents perhaps the most unpredicted period of ever-worsening, non-hot war inflation yet.

The Path to an 2 Inflationary Recession

President John Kennedy had pledged his administration to get America moving. Fortunately, he inherited an economic recovery. He was lucky because the independent Federal Reserve system under Chairman William McChesney Martin decided to help foster the recovery by injecting more money into circulation than it had been doing in the past. The Fed (as it is usually called) controls the total amount of dollar bills and checking account balances outstanding via its control over banks' reserves. When the Fed wants to increase the money supply, it helps build up bank reserves by buying financial assets from the public and the banks. To pay for those bonds, the Fed merely writes a check against itself or simply jots down the amount owed a bank in that bank's reserve account. Banks which then have higher reserves can go out and buy other interest producing assets. One way that they do this is to loan money for a fee to people like you and us or to businessmen.

The shift in monetary policy in late 1960 may have caused the bottoming out of the recession that Kennedy had inherited from the Eisenhower administration. In any event, it was

4

the 1960-61 recession that put the U.S. in shape for the long recovery to follow.

The large increase in output from 1961 to 1965 was possible because there were unemployed men and machines when the expansion started. During this period wage rates continued to expand at a fairly slow pace, because of substantial unemployment. Consequently the increase in GNP (at 6.8 percent annually), resulting in part from a moderate expansion in the money supply (at a 3 percent annual rate), occurred primarily as an expansion of output rather than inflation. The rate of inflation averaged only 1.4 percent a year.

In 1965, the money supply growth rate accelerated to a 6.6 percent annual rate, partly to finance escalated military expenditures in Vietnam. As could be expected, the gross national product also accelerated. As a result of the rapid expansion in employment since 1961, the economy reached one of those rare moments of almost full employment. Because of full employment, no more than the existing growth in real output was possible. The burst of GNP growth during 1965 and 1966 therefore had to occur mostly in the form of rising prices. The economy was up against the wall of available productive capacity.

This acceleration of inflation scared the Federal Reserve into slowing down the rate of monetary growth. Some observers have called this episode "the Fed's finest hour" because it demonstrated the Fed's independence of the President, a fact long bemoaned by chief executives. President Johnson vigorously protested this slowdown in the rate of monetary growth. In fact, the President called William McChesney Martin, then Chairman of the Board of Governors of the Federal Reserve System, down to the Ranch to persuade him to change his monetary policy. However, Martin resisted the suasions of barbequed steaks and Texas hospitality; the Federal Reserve remained determined to slow the rate of monetary growth, and that it did. During the last three quarters of 1966 the money supply actually *fell* slightly, to the horror of the administration. The mini-recession of late 1966 and early 1967 was the result,[1] with GNP growth slowing drastically. However, prices continued to rise at over 2.5 percent because of wage increases induced by expectations of continuing inflation; therefore output only expanded at a piddling 0.6 percent annual rate. Unemployment started to rise, much to the chagrin of the Fed.

Just as the Federal Reserve had overreacted to the inflation in 1965, now it overreacted to the rise in unemployment. In its panic-stricken state, it caused the money supply to skyrocket at the extremely rapid rate of 7.6 percent a year from 1967 to 1969. The result was an inflation that we are still trying to contain. By 1969 prices were rising at over 6 percent a year.

One would think the Fed was having a hard time keeping the nation's supply of circulating money under control. Such is not the case. The Fed may end up not being able to manage the economy the way it would like, but it has complete and total control over the money supply by its ability to change available and required bank reserves.

In 1969 the Federal Reserve finally restrained the rate of monetary growth in two steps. From January to July of 1969, the annual rate of growth in the money supply was reduced to 5.1 percent. Then, from July to December of 1969, even more drastic measures were taken, and the money supply growth rate slowed substantially to a mere 0.6 percent annually. Following that significant decrease in the rate of growth in the money supply, the slowdown in economic activity beginning in the fourth quarter of 1969 was to be expected. Even when total spending slows down, there is usually a lag before inflation starts to slow. Workers and businessmen think good times will continue so workers demand higher wages and businessmen think they can grant them and just pass the cost on to customers without any loss in sales. Since prices continued to rise at about 6 percent a year, output had to fall and unemployment had to increase.

Then, on January 31, 1970 Arthur Burns became Chairman of the Federal Reserve Board of Governors. He quickly

[1] Businessmen found out how important long-established dealings with one bank were during this "credit crunch."

changed monetary policy to one of moderate growth, and the economy was set up for another about-face. From February 1970 to January 1971 the Federal Reserve increased the money supply at about a 6 percent annual rate. At the same time growth in GNP accelerated and output started to expand again. It looked like labor and business might have reason to rejoice, but the expansion was a moderate one, not vigorous enough to reduce the unemployment rate. The Federal Reserve faced the cruel dilemma of choosing between higher inflation and high unemployment in early 1971. President Nixon was understandably uneasy about the effects of lingering unemployment on his 1972 election. The Federal Reserve was therefore under not so subtle pressure to do something even more stimulating to the laggard economy. Evidently the Fed responded to that pressure because the money supply increased an almost unprecedented 10 percent a year during the first half of 1971.

Until the summer of 1971 the Nixon economic game plan relied on an increase in people's total desire to spend to stimulate employment and output. GNP rose quite rapidly during the first half of 1971. Unfortunately, most of that increase in total spending was due simply to rising prices, which is a rather undesirable state of affairs. This happened for a simple but usually neglected reason. The inflationary expectations generated by 4 years of rising prices and wages were sufficient to sustain continued high rates of inflation despite an unemployment rate of over 6 percent. Workers, expecting the future to reflect the past, raised their wage demands to protect their purchasing power even though unemployment was high. Those who had jobs were successful. Producers, in turn, passed the increased labor costs on to consumers, as all of us can painfully testify. Higher prices, though, reduce the demand for final output. As sales fall off, producers are not likely to increase employment and output. Therefore, it was the rising labor costs which caused the increases in GNP to take the form of higher prices and not greater output.

Many Democrats had vociferously suggested an alternative to Nixon's game plan. Even Richard Nixon's long-standing economic counselor Arthur Burns advocated some sort of control on wages and prices. On December 1, 1970 Chairman Burns gave a speech at Pepperdine College in Los Angeles in which he reversed his former objections to wage and price ceilings. Burns voiced his doubts that even an expansion of total spending could be sufficient to generate an acceptable recovery. He also feared that an unacceptable rate of inflation would be an inevitable side effect of the necessary rise in GNP. Arthur Burns therefore urged the President to create a voluntary wage and price review board to curb the wage-price spiral.

Nixon felt deserted and continued to deny the need for such a drastic policy. Growth in productivity was increasing at a healthy rate and all that was needed was a little time for inflationary expectations to cool down, he replied. Unemployed workers would become reasonable; they would soon realize that there were few jobs available at the higher wage rates demanded, and would reduce their excessive wage demands. The whole team pulled together as George Shultz, Director of the Office of Management and the Budget, and Dr. Paul McCracken, Chairman of the Council of Economic Advisers, continued to argue against controls in their advice to the President and in the press.[2]

In early July 1971 Treasury Secretary Connally was sent out by the President to tell reporters the economy "is expanding beyond any question," and since progress has been made "in slowing the rate of inflation:

> No. 1, he isn't going to institute a wage price review board.
> No. 2, he isn't going to impose mandatory wage and price controls.
> No. 3, he isn't going to ask Congress for any tax relief.
> No. 4, he isn't going to increase fiscal spending.

But by August 1971 Secretary of the Treasury John Con-

[2] Paul McCracken's scathing rebuttal to testimony by Harvard Professor John K. Galbraith before the Joint Economic Committee, during which the Cambridge economist pleaded, as usual, for freezing all prices, appears in Chapter 5.

nally and the President were disturbed that the marketplace was not adjusting to the Nixon game plan as expected. Renegade industries, such as steel, continued to raise prices despite excess capacity. Ungrateful unions with high levels of unemployment in their ranks obstinately persisted in demanding large wage increases. The economies of many sections of the United States were paralyzed by bitter strikes, such as that which hit West Coast shipping. A strike in the steel industry was narrowly averted by a last minute wage settlement which amounted to a 31 percent increase over a period of 3 years, causing an enormous 8 percent across-the-board price hike for that product. Disaster piled upon economic disaster. The public mood seemed to demand an immediate solution to the wage-price spiral. A distraught and defeated President Nixon finally accepted Arthur Burns's advice. He sadly imposed a temporary freeze on all wages and prices. But as a wise Washington commentator once said: "The effectiveness of a politician varies inversely to his commitment to principle."

A Little History 3
of Controlled Prices

Presumably Nixon knew what he was getting into. The history of gimmicks to keep prices and wages from rising is rather well known. In a *Playboy* interview some years ago, Professor John Kenneth Galbraith told about his days with the Office of Price Administration during World War II. At one point in the interview, Dr. Galbraith said he had decided during one trying moment in those wartorn years that it might be easier for a price of $5.00 to be set on *everything*. Such a radical idea is proof enough that the job of keeping the lid on prices during World War II must not have been easy.

In World War II the pressure of huge government expenditures (initially a large share was paid for by increasing the money supply) and full employment were sure to bring about rising prices. Congress was only willing to raise taxes to cover 61 percent of its expenditures. The Price Control Act of January 1942 established the Office of Price Administration. By mid-1943 fully 95 percent of the nation's foodstuffs were rationed and maximum prices and rents had been established. The Anti-inflation Act of October 1942 established the Office of Economic Stabilization. Its purpose was to limit any wages and salaries and curb any prices and rents that had escaped the clutches of the other organization. At the height of price controls, these two offices, along with the Office of War Mobilization created in 1943, were aided by about 400,000 paid and volunteer "price watchers" scattered throughout the country. (One never knew when someone would turn him in for seeking out a black market "profiteer" to get more than the ration tickets allowed.) This enormous nationwide effort resulted in wholesale prices rising only 14 percent from November 1941 to August 1945.[1]

The U.S. was not the only country to feel that the national emergency of war necessitated drastic measures. Nazi Germany also controlled prices. So-called economic crimes, such as selling products above the maximum legal price, were immediately dealt with in a very harsh manner. When the Allies occupied Germany after the war, they didn't dismantle the rationing scheme though they did soften the punishment somewhat. It was felt that pandemonium would have broken out in an already chaotic situation. For 3 years, strict price controls remained in effect. But something very strange was happening. Available money in circulation increased a phenomenal 400 percent, while output fell by 50 percent. It was inevitable that barter should develop as the mark became useless for obtaining goods and services because of widespread shortages. Believe it or not, American cigarettes became the unofficial currency.

Obviously, price controls in occupied Germany were much more "successful" than in postwar America. They were so successful that the official price index hardly budged at all.

It is interesting also to note what happened in post-World War I Germany. The Allies, using the Treaty of Versailles, had imposed immense reparation payments on that war-torn

---

[1] However, when the war and controls ended the story changed. The wholesale price index jumped 55 percent from August 1945 to August 1948.

country. In order to finance these payments the Weimar Republic printed marks—lots of them. By 1923 the German government was spending 12 *billion* marks more than it was receiving in taxes. Its expenditures were 7 times as great as its revenues. The mark-U.S. dollar exchange rate went from 14 to 1 in 1919 to 4,200,000,000 to 1 in 1923! Since there weren't any price controls then, retail prices and wages adjusted rapidly to the influx of marks. In the end there were *hourly* changes in prices!

In contrast to the reduction in output in post-World War II Germany, output in post-World War I Germany did not fall until the last 6 months of that country's hyperinflation. At that time people got tired of pushing a wheelbarrow full of marks to the store just to buy a knockwurst. They finally resorted to barter.

The juxtaposition of these periods in German history demonstrates what can happen during periods of phenomenal increases in the amount of money in circulation—with and without price controls.

If the money supply increases rapidly, the public's attempts to get rid of excess money balances produce excess demand for goods and services. Market prices will rise until people no longer want to decrease their average cash and checking account balances. If price controls prevent prices from rising, the excess demand for goods and services becomes apparent as shortages develop. At the legal price level, the demand for goods will exceed the supply of goods, requiring an alternative method of rationing the available supply. After all, individuals hold money balances in order to have a liquid stock of purchasing power over goods and services. If there are widespread shortages due to excess demand for goods and services, money no longer serves as a liquid stock of purchasing power over goods and services. Money balances can no longer perform the services for which they were held. The resort to barter or the creation of a new commodity currency, such as cigarettes, naturally follows.

A good contemporary example is in South America. When Chile's new Marxist President Allende simultaneously raised wages and froze prices in one stroke of his governmental pen, appliance stores were empty within a short time. Chileans didn't want to keep the increased cash they ended up with, so they quickly went on a spending spree. Since prices couldn't rise in response, the spree stopped when stocks of goods were depleted.

Back in post-World War II Germany there essentially was a complete destruction of the monetary standard because people couldn't get any goods with their money. After price controls were lifted, a new banking system was instituted and the Marshall Plan got rolling. West Germany then experienced what has been called a miracle. Between 1948 and 1964 industrial production increased *600 percent!* Real GNP tripled between 1950 and 1964. Per capita GNP in real terms increased faster in West Germany than in any other Western European or North American country. Of course this experience was a "miracle" only to those who were not initiated into the mysteries of economics. Astute readers know the real cause.

There has been little support since the forties for full-fledged price controls in this country, except for a brief while during the Korean conflict. The concept of informal guidelines or guideposts has been given a lot of attention, though. Every *Economic Report of the President and the Council of Economic Advisers* since 1957 has stressed, in one form or another, that private pricing discretion should be tempered to create stable prices. Restraint on the part of business and workers has been politely requested as the government hoped that people would consider national interest over profits. The 1960 *Economic Report* was explicit in stating that wage increases should not exceed the growth in average *national* productivity. It further suggested that price reductions were called for in sectors experiencing exceptionally rapid productivity growth.

The 1962 *Report* went even further. It gave us a formal statement of guideposts for wage increases stating that they should not exceed about 3.5 percent, which was the rate of growth of productivity in the economy.

Many other countries have attempted to use some form of guideposts in order to insure price stability and high employ-ment. Holland started a program immediately after World War II. A Foundation of Labor was established as a forum for continual discussion of national wage policy. For about 6 years unions went along with the system that tied money wages to the cost of living. By the mid-1950s, increasing total aggregate demand caused employers to start bidding workers away from each other at successively higher wages. In order to skirt official guideposts, employers started to increase fringe benefits and upgrade workers so that they could be paid higher wages without formally deviating from the guide-posts. By the late fifties and throughout the sixties unem-ployment was extremely low in the Netherlands. Major em-ployers overtly refused to hold wage offers within the legal ceiling. In 1959 the Dutch government decided to peg wage increases to productivity in different industries. The system suffered a total collapse in 1964 and 1965. Professor John Sheahan noted that "the Dutch experience has been cited as a leading example of the failure of negotiated agreements to hold down wages in conditions of excess demand, despite all the advantages of centralized bargaining, recognized concern for the balance of payments, and sophisticated economic forecasting. The point cannot be disputed."[2]

In the sixties the French government's response to the rise in unit labor costs in manufacturing was a general freeze in September 1963. This price stabilization program was not part of a general integrated set of policies until it was includ-ed in the fifth plan covering 1966-70. The French approach involved explicit decisions on how different types of income should grow during that period. For example, it was decided that the real wages of workers should go up at 3.3 percent a year and agricultural income at 4.8 percent a year. An exam-ple of pure Cartesian logic.

France's incomes policy worked as well as could be expect-ed. As Gardner Ackley, former Chairman of the Council of

[2]P. 102. *The Wage-Price Guideposts*, The Brookings Institution, Wash-ington, D.C., 1967.

Economic Advisers, said: "In almost all cases, the policy has sooner or later broken down, followed by an upward surge of wages and prices." France's incomes policy came to an abrupt end in May 1968's near revolution, modestly called "les évenements de mai."

And still other countries have had similarly poor luck with an incomes policy. In late 1970, about the time when Arthur Burns first proposed a wage and price review board, the Canadians were abandoning their wage and price controls. Canada's wage and price controls did not work because labor simply ignored them. Prices were pegged in the face of rising labor costs. This situation contributed to a 6.6 percent unemployment rate in Canada.

The idea behind such wage and price controls is held to be self-evident: a country can thus have higher rates of employment without the odious consequences of rising prices. While the debate is not yet exhausted on this idea, there is a place for guidelines consistent with a theory about the adjustment period between rising prices and stable prices.

Monetary and fiscal policy from 1967 to 1969 was extremely expansionary. It abruptly changed in 1969. Not until early 1971 did the government really start priming the pump again. During this period of adjustment and concomitant high unemployment, people still expected high rates of inflation. After all, businessmen had learned to expect that they could raise prices without decreasing sales. Union workers had just suffered a period of little *real* change in wages. Everyone would have found it very difficult to suddenly accept the idea that there was a permanent decrease in the growth of nominal aggregate demand.

Here's where guidelines and freezes might logically come in. If they were to be established in order to signal a *permanent* change in government monetary and fiscal policy which would be consistent with a stable price level, then wage and price controls could have the effect of accelerating the *adjustment of expectations* to the new price stability.

However, the structure of prices would probably be seriously distorted by price- and wage-fixing legislation, producing shortages of some goods and misallocation of resources. The best method for speeding up the adjustment of expectations to changing rates of inflation would be contracts negotiated in *real* terms rather than *nominal* terms. Workers and management could sign contracts linking wage rates to a cost of living index, thus eliminating the problems associated with forecasting future inflation. Wages would then go up rapidly only if there were inflation. If prices remained stable, the rise in wage rates would simply reflect the agreed upon growth in real purchasing power. The authors feel that the use of such contracts would contribute significantly to stable growth in output. They could virtually eliminate the phenomenon of an inflationary recession such as the one which caused Nixon and his advisors to opt for a wage and price freeze and then for continued selective controls on major industries "where price and wage behavior influences the whole economy."

Nixon's 90-Day Freeze, **4** or How To Stump the Democrats

Paul McCracken, the Chairman of the Council of Economic Advisers, wrote the following article in the Washington Post in rebuttal of John Kenneth Galbraith's testimony before the Joint Economic Committee, during which the Harvard economist pleaded again for freezing all prices.

Galbraith and price-wage controls*
In his recent testimony before the Joint Economic Committee, the noted Democratic economist J. K. Galbraith again offered the country his remedy for its economic problems. The remedy is wage and price controls, now and forever. His prescription has the merit of being logical within the limits of his peculiar view of the economic system. He has been making clear for at least the past 20 years his scorn for the idea that prices serve to guide the economic system into producing what consumers want. Believing that prices are only labels stuck on real things with no other function than to extract income from consumers, Galbraith, of course, has no hesitation about "interfering" with these prices.

*Reprinted from *The Washington Post*, July 28, 1971

This view of the function of prices, and how to keep them from being "too high" was, of course, common for centuries until people began to study the question with some theoretical rigor and empirical evidence. It is still common among uneducated people. Galbraith's view is unusual only in being held by the president of the American Economic Association and in being described by him as new.

Having no use for what others call the price system, Galbraith does not fool around making bows to it. Others who want to restrain wages and prices talk about voluntary and temporary "income policies." These would, allegedly, not really keep anyone from doing what he badly wanted to do; they never diverge far from what a competitive market would produce; and they would be over before they could do much damage. However, Galbraith goes at once to the logical conclusion of this line of thought. He wants an immediate, comprehensive, mandatory wage-price freeze to be followed later by permanent price and wage controls on the largest corporations and unions.

Well, why not? Haven't we all, and not least the Council of Economic Advisers, had enough of the endless sea of troubles that this inflation is, and should we not end them at a stroke with the clear, sure weapon of controls? The temptation is great, especially if someone else will administer the controls. But the temptation must be resisted, for several cogent reasons:

1. Despite Galbraith's dismissal of it, the adjustment of prices in the market does contribute to the efficiency of production and its adaptation to the desires of consumers. U.S. experience with general price control in wartime and with limited price controls in regulated industries shows the loss of consumer satisfaction that results. Observation of the pattern of production in other countries that have suppressed the price system confirms this conclusion. The tendency in the European socialist countries to increase reliance on market prices is evidence for it.

2. General price and wage control would be a serious threat to individual freedom. It is amazing that the press, so jealous of its own freedom, does not recognize what would be the implications of having the income of literally everyone in the country controlled by a government agency. In World War II, newspapers were exempted from price control to avoid the possibility of infringing on the freedom of the press. Does wage control violate the Constitutional ban on involuntary servitude?

3. The common image of price-wage control is entirely wrong. The image is that a little band of dedicated, objective, analytical men in Washington would keep a few heads of powerful corporations and unions from exploiting "us." The fact is that it is "us" who would be and would have to be controlled. And the control would not be managed by Moses, or Buddha, or Galbraith (at least not forever) but by the same kind of people who run and operate all the other agencies in Washington. That is to say, they would be political and bureaucratic.

As an aid to realistic thinking about the problem of price control, I list in the accompanying table the items in the consumer price index that rose most in the last year.

Biggest increases in the consumer price index June 1970 to June 1971

Item	% increase
Carrots	40.5
Green peppers	30.4
Postal charges	25.3
Cucumbers	22.5
Lettuce	19.6
Dried beans	16.6
Canned sardines	15.8
Fish, fresh or frozen	14.2
Reshingling roofs	13.9
Canned tunafish	13.5
Residential water and sewage charges	13.4
Semi-private hospital room	13.2
Oranges	13.2
Bus fares, intercity	13.0
Watermelon	13.0
Auto insurance rates	12.6
Private hospital room	12.4
Washing machine repairs	12.2
Repainting living room	12.1
Taxicab fares	11.9
Cracker meal	11.8
Airplane fare, chiefly coach	10.8
Railroad fare, coach	10.6
Fruit cocktail	10.5
Newspapers	10.2
Replacing sinks	10.0

4. The idea of a freeze is illusory. Wages and prices would be in upward motion from the first day. Millions of workers are covered by contracts that call for wage increases still to come. But profit margins are very low. If these wage increases already contracted for are granted, prices will have to rise. But then other wages will have to rise, as a result of escalator clauses or otherwise. In fact, the whole process may be inflationary because the standards for prices and wages that must be established in order to assure cooperation and "equity" may raise rather than lower inflationary expectations.

5. Wage-price controls threaten to speed up inflation from the demand side also. These controls, or less rigorous forms of incomes policy, are now commonly proposed as part of a package. One half of the package is restraint on prices and wages and the other half is pumping the economy quickly up to full employment by tax cuts or expenditure increases or both. The expansionist part of the package is easy and popular; the restraint part will be neither. Only a little common sense is required to forecast the relative strengths of the restraint part and the expansion part of the package. After all, the Johnson Administration had its two-part package also—guideposts for restraint, and fiscal policy for expansion. The expansion ran away with the restraint.

Because he is so logical, the difference between Professor Galbraith and the Nixon Administration on this matter is clear. Believing that the price system contributes nothing to the well-being of the American people he is prepared to suppress it. Believing that the price system has a major part in the high standard of living and economic satisfaction of the American people, we are determined to strengthen it.

Being a novelist and wit, Galbraith can dismiss the problems of carrying out the policy he proposes. Being government officials, we cannot.

Being a Democratic partisan, he can proclaim that we are now in an economic crisis. Being the successors to a Democratic Administration, we feel relief at having averted the crisis to which the policies of our predecessors were tending.

During the historic meeting at Camp David, on August 14 and 15, 1971, the same Paul W. McCracken who wrote this biting article was put in charge of the details of the wage-price freeze. The ironies of history!

Could it work? Can wages and prices be frozen in the face

of expanding total spending? Remember that the Federal Reserve had increased the money supply at an annual rate of more than 10 percent during the first half of 1971. That rapid expansion in the money supply should have produced large increases in total spending during the last half of 1971 and early 1972. If effectively enforced, the freeze would have eliminated inflation during that 90-day period. But when prices cannot rise in response to increased total spending, consumers will demand more final output. The Nixon administration hoped that this increase in demand for final output could be satisfied by increased production. We know, though, that when output does not increase sufficiently to satisfy that increased demand, shortages will develop. The success of Nixon's wage-price freeze depended critically on whether sufficient output would be forthcoming at the controlled prices to prevent shortages from developing. A prevention of shortages in turn is dependent upon a sufficient supply of labor available at controlled wage rates and the presence of producer incentives to increase output.

Was there reason to believe that there would be a net supply of labor forthcoming at the controlled wage rate? The answer depends in great measure on the expectations held by unemployed workers. Much of today's unemployment results from a lengthening of the average duration of unemployment. Unemployed workers reject job offers and continue searching for additional job offers because they anticipate receiving higher wage rates. The wage freeze held wage rates at the then current level offered by employers. Whenever the wage freeze psychologically discouraged workers from holding out for better wages, workers probably accepted jobs earlier, thus reducing the average duration of unemployment.

Unfortunately, it seems just as likely that unemployed workers may have had just the reverse reaction. If they expected an increase in the level of wage offers after the freeze, unemployed workers may have rejected job offers during the freeze period. This response would tend to reduce the supply of labor forthcoming at the controlled wage rates.

Moreover, the current unemployment rate may be misleading as an indicator of the actual labor force which can be quickly reemployed. Labor shortages may occur in many sectors of the economy while unemployment is still quite high. Much of the current unemployment is sectoral. The economic priorities of government spending have drastically changed during the Nixon administration, with the defense industry, especially aerospace, losing much government business as a result both of the wind down of the War in Indochina and taxpayer disfavor. Current unemployment, therefore, has not been as evenly distributed geographically as it had been in other recessions. It has been highly concentrated in defense industry cities such as Seattle and Los Angeles. Such structural unemployment makes it difficult to reduce the unemployment rate below 5 percent very quickly. For example, engineers and other technical workers in the defense industries have to be retrained if they are to earn comparable wage rates in other industries.[1] In addition, the character of the labor force has changed. There are far more teenagers and women working and seeking jobs than in the past decade. These categories of employees typically have higher than average unemployment rates since they are "the first fired and the last hired."

The supply of labor is only half of the problem. The question of whether employers have an incentive to hire workers and increase output at a controlled price level is also relevant. Producers are interested, of course, in maximizing their profits. As long as the increased labor costs of hiring additional employees are less than the increased revenue their new employment generates, it is profitable to expand output and increase employment. When wages and prices are frozen, the productivity of the additional workers employed will determine the profitability of their employment. Nixon counted on labor's productivity being high enough to make further employment profitable. *Capital available*

It turns out that one of the most important factors in determining the productivity of additional workers is the capital available for them to work with. When the capital stock is already being fully utilized, additional workers will

---

[1] If not, they often choose to remain unemployed.

not be very productive. Fortunately for Nixon, then, the current excess capacity in the economy could keep the productivity of additional workers high.

One other factor leading to the success of a temporary freeze during the early part of recovery from a recession is that output can be increased even without large increases in employment. This is true because employers essentially hold an inventory of labor—i.e., employees temporarily kept on the payroll even though they aren't currently needed for production. The labor costs of keeping these extra workers on the payroll are offset by the costs of rehiring or losing them to other employers if they are laid off.

Because of this already existing inventory of labor and of substantial unemployed men and machines, no noticeable widespread shortages occurred within Nixon's 90 days, but if the all-inclusive wage-price freeze had continued far into 1972, shortages undoubtedly would occur. Perhaps sensing what might happen, the President promised that the freeze would end in 90 days. Nixon opted for a system of "No. 2 phase" curbs on major industries. The country would return to a free economy soon, Nixon promised, but until inflation is licked "we feel it is necessary to have controls backed up by teeth, made effective by the government." When first announcing the Phase 2 system, Nixon said that it would provide for "adjustment of inequities." We predict that the most important adjustments that the politically-minded presidential incumbent will make will occur in those price controlled industries which began to experience shortages.

It is interesting to note that George Meany, President of the AFL-CIO, demanded that any wage controls after the 90-day period be accompanied by a ceiling on interest rates and a freeze on profits. This seemingly heroic demand ignores the fact that profits have been in the past few years extremely low by historical standards. Corporate profits are 30 percent below the level they would be if they had maintained the share of GNP that they averaged for the last 10 years. In fact, the share of GNP going to corporate profits is the lowest it has been in more than 30 years. If the wage-price freeze were to extend to profits, the results could be disastrous, because such a move would destroy all incentive for business to expand employment and output. It is extremely naive to depend on business "charity" to provide new jobs.

Another rather naive suggestion made by the labor leader was a call for a freeze on dividends. If dividends are frozen, corporations can simply invest the earnings which would have been paid out in dividends. The increased net worth of the corporation will result in an appreciation of stock prices. Stockholders will receive their returns in capital gains rather than in dividends. In fact, this is one of the principles of growth stocks. So it really matters little whether dividends are frozen or not.

Ultimately, the rate of monetary growth during the rest of 1971 and during 1972 will determine to a large extent whether or not inflation diminishes. If the rapid money supply growth experienced during the first half of 1971 continues, the inflation will accelerate in one form or another no matter what kind of wage and price controls are tried. In fact, under those conditions, wage and price controls can only create shortages. When the controls are lifted, inflation will return.

But even if the wage-price freeze did not cure our inflationary recession, it probably will not be a political liability in the 1972 election since it was first advocated by the Democrats. President Nixon launched a risky program with which few of his own advisers agreed in the past, but which none of his Democratic opponents opposed.

Tax Credits and 5
Job Development

"I will propose to provide the strongest short-term incentive in our history to invest in new machinery and equipment that will create new jobs for Americans: a 10 percent Job Development Credit for one year, effective as of today, with a 5 percent credit after August 15, 1972. This tax credit for investment in new equipment will not only generate new jobs, it will raise productivity and it will make our goods more competitive in the years ahead."

Thus Richard Nixon's new economics involved proposing a reinstatement of an investment tax credit that John Kennedy had convinced Congress to enact in 1962. That "permanent" 7 percent credit was removed from the books in 1969. The 10 percent job development tax credit that Nixon proposed is merely equal to 20 percent additional depreciation on long-lived U.S.-built capital assets purchased during the time the credit is to be in effect. This is so because the credit is against corporate income tax liabilities. Therefore, given that the current corporate tax rate is around 50 percent, the

10 percent credit is strictly equivalent to business being able to write off an extra 20 percent the year a machine is purchased.

Certain effects of any such tax credit are immediately obvious. To the extent that this tax credit does not apply equally to all assets, there will be a shifting of resources in the economy. For example, the job development credit does not apply to assets which have service lives of less than 8 years. There will be relatively more investment in longer-lived than shorter-lived capital when this credit is made into law. In addition, the credit does not apply to consumer durables, housing in particular. There will be relatively less investment in housing and other consumer durables and relatively more in producer durables. Moreover the credit does not apply to foreign-made capital. Therefore there will be a shift away from foreign-made to domestically made producer durables.

In any event, an investment tax credit increases the profitability of new investment opportunities. The financing of these new investment opportunities which have become profitable because of the tax credit will tend to increase market rates of interest, everything else remaining the same. Businessmen will demand more loanable funds and, with any given supply available, the price of those loanable funds (credit) will have to rise.

If we consider the investment tax credit in isolation, it can only mean one thing for the government in the short run— less tax revenues. The Nixon program outlined on August 15, 1971 did not forget about this point because his proposal also involved substantial decreases in government spending, even to the extent of overmatching those decreased tax revenues. In the past when such fiscal schemes were presented, a concomitant decrease in government spending was not proposed. This was true of Kennedy's 1962 investment tax credit.

The obvious idea behind such a tax credit is to stimulate the producer durable industry and thereby cause a chain reaction in the rest of the economy, increasing employment and output everywhere. Such a view of the economy is naive and incomplete because it ignores the decreased tax revenues on the part of the Federal Government commensurate with the institution of the investment tax credit. How does the government make up these tax losses? That is a key question ignored by numerous economic analysts.

If the loss in tax revenues is made up by money created by the Federal Reserve, then the so-called tax stimulus ends up being a trigger for monetary expansion, something that could be done without any new fiscal stimuli. On the other hand, if the lost tax revenues are made up by increased borrowing on the part of the federal government, the end result, on aggregate demand, may be imperceptible.

Although the argument supporting this last statement is somewhat subtle and complex, it is worth going over. The way the government borrows is by selling bonds to the public. The private sector, in order to maintain its desired money balances, must reduce expenditures sufficiently to permit the purchase of those bonds. Further, if government spending follows the same course it was going to, and the lost tax revenues due to the investment tax credit are made up by selling bonds, taxpayers will have to pay higher taxes in the future to cover the interest payments on these bonds. If enough people are aware of this fact (and they might not be, at least not in the short run), then they will increase their savings in order to pay the higher taxes in the future. When businessmen go to banks to get more loanable funds in order to finance new investment made possible by the institution of the investment tax credit, they will find that the supply of funds has therefore risen and they need not pay higher interest rates to get those funds. If this is the case, then there will merely have been a shifting of resources in the economy with no change in desired total aggregate spending.

Economists who support such fiscal measures as the investment tax credit obviously do not think that people will be able to understand that lost tax revenues made up by the government's selling bonds increases their taxes in the future. If so, consumers are incorrectly discounting their future tax liabilities. They will not increase their savings, and therefore when businessmen go to borrow funds, the supply will be inadequate and the interest rate will rise. That is, the price of credit will rise. Fiscal policy advocates maintain that when the price of credit—the interest rate—rises, people will want to spend more money. The reason they will want to spend more money is that the cost of holding cash will have gone up; people will attempt to get rid of some of this cash. For example, if the interest rate rises from 5 percent to 10 percent it will now cost every individual 10¢ a year to hold $1 in a checking account. Rather than hold this dollar in a checking account or in the form of currency, the individual may choose to spend it.

Obviously this subtle argument was not foremost in the minds of the policy makers who helped the President formulate his new game plan. In fact, one leading fiscal policy advocate, Dr. George Perry of the Brookings Institution, quickly went on record predicting that the fiscal stimulus provided by Nixon's program would not be big if that program were enacted *intact*. The Nixon plan involved both programs which would result in government spending cuts and programs which would result in tax revenue losses. The tax cuts would total $6.3 billion in fiscal 1972, and the spending cuts would total $4.7 billion. In addition there would be $2.1 billion of *increased* tax receipts from the import surtax, which we will discuss in following chapters. The government would come out about $500 million ahead as a result of the whole program. Few fiscal policy advocates would consider that as stimulating the economy.

Nonetheless forecasters of the U.S. economy immediately came forth with glowing predictions about the effects of the Nixon program. Michael K. Evans, President of Chase Econometrics Associates, estimated that the implementation of the Nixon plan would create 750,000 jobs for the troubled economy. At that time we failed to see the reasoning behind such an ebullient outlook. It was true that the specific tax cuts which Nixon proposed would result in substantial employment increases in certain sectors. The automobile industry most certainly would experience an increase in employment due to the lower relative and absolute price of American cars. Along with a repeal of the 7 percent excise tax on automobiles, Nixon raised the tariff on imported cars from 3.5 percent to 10 percent. It looked like Vegas would start being a better bargain than Toyotas and Datsuns. Nixon went on record maintaining that for every increase in sales of 100,000 cars there would be an additional 25,000 workers hired by GM, Ford, Chrysler, and American Motors.

And, to be sure, a decrease in personal taxes as proposed by Nixon would give consumers more income to spend. But, as we mentioned above, that is not the end of the story. We have to look at the complete situation. On the one hand, the government gives consumers more income to spend, but on the other hand, it does not collect as many tax dollars. Since, at the same time, Nixon proposed substantial cuts in government spending, the net effect on employment might have ended up being zero. And certainly the net effect on employment would be much less than anticipated. The idea behind fiscal stimulus is for the government to effect a *net* reduction in taxes or, what amounts to the same thing, a net increase in government spending. Nixon's program wouldn't have done either.

Nixon's new economic program was not, therefore, designed to add significantly to total aggregate demand. However, although much less noticed and certainly even less understood, his program was designed to change the structure of total spending through his use of taxes. The investment tax credit, the repeal of the automobile excise tax, and the import surcharge were all aimed at inducing consumers to spend more for some products and less on others. In the past, stimulative monetary and fiscal policies have usually been concentrated in consumer durable industry, particularly housing. Nixon's new program, on the other hand, was designed to increase spending in the producer durable and automobile sectors. And for a very good reason.

By mid-1971 unemployment in the auto capital of the world, Detroit, had reached 14 percent. Forecasts for the year were for only 8 to 8.5 million new cars. Foreign imports were accounting for over 18 percent of new car sales. In some cities, such as Los Angeles, foreign imports accounted for many times that amount in new car sales. The repeal of the excise tax on automobiles definitely improved the price competitiveness of cars relative to other goods.[1] In addition, the increase in taxes on foreign cars improved the price competitiveness of domestic as opposed to foreign automobiles.

The stock market reacted strongly to Nixon's program. The owners of American Motors, for example, experienced a 30 percent appreciation in the value of their stock virtually overnight.

The producer goods sector was experiencing excess capacity because of the recession and the previous repeal of the investment tax credit in 1969. Particularly hard hit were machine tool and computer industries. They had experienced a drastic drop in sales. The reinvestment of the investment tax credit would stimulate spending in these sectors. Moreover, domestic producer durables would have an overwhelming competitive advantage over foreign imports because of the 10 percent import surcharge. Further, they would benefit from the fact that the investment tax credit would not apply to imported producer durables.

---

[1] It is interesting to note that Nixon was willing to increase employment in the automobile industry by causing over-all demand for new cars to rise. At the same time, his Council on Environmental Quality was lamenting the destruction of the ecology caused by the automobile.

"I am Now a Keynesian" 6
—Richard Nixon, 1971

Nixon announced he was a Keynesian. One of Spiro Agnew's aides said that the Vice President was also a Keynesian. Professor Milton Friedman of the University of Chicago was even misquoted as saying "We are all Keynesians now."

What's in a label? In this case, it is nothing more than an appeal to a famous and respected figure in economic theory. Keynes is cited as an authority in what is basically a debate about the empirical effects of fiscal policy actions—government spending—not accompanied by expansion of money in circulation. Until the Great Depression very few economists believed that fiscal policy alone could be an effective way to stimulate total spending. Although economists generally accepted the proposition that government spending financed by money creation would increase total spending, they doubted that such a program financed by taxing or borrowing would achieve the same effect. They believed that the financing of government spending by taxing or borrowing would simply "crowd out" (reduce) private expenditures by an amount roughly equal to the increase in government spending.

The apparent ineffectiveness of monetary policy during

those gloomy years from 1929 to the start of World War II convinced many young economists and even a few older ones that monetary policy was not a useful tool for stabilizing aggregate output. This interpretation of the facts was largely based upon the error of using interest rates as indicators of monetary policy. The Federal Reserve has a habit of judging the effects of its monetary policy by market rates of interest. The low interest rates during the thirties, resulting from the collapse of investment opportunities, were regarded by the Fed as proof of the success of their efforts to stimulate the economy through "easy" money. This erroneous interpretation misled economists into concluding that monetary policy was ineffective.

Actually there was a violent *contraction* of the money supply from 1929 to 1933, when it fell by over 30 percent. Recovery was halted by an additional contraction in 1937. At the time, however, money supply statistics were not readily available. It was not until the early 1950s that the Federal Reserve started collecting accurate figures on the nation's total supply of currency and demand deposits. Current statistical data gathering techniques still do not yield very accurate figures on the stock of money in the U.S. The Federal Reserve has been forced to change its money supply time series data at least three times in the past 3 years. The tragic misjudgment of monetary policy in the thirties points up the importance of collecting accurate statistics on the money aggregates.

Into this atmosphere of doubt and confusion concerning the ability of monetary policy to stimulate growth in total spending came *The General Theory of Employment, Interest and Money* (1936) by John Maynard Keynes. In brief, Keynes demonstrated theoretically that fiscal policy could be used as an alternative to monetary policy to stimulate total spending. Keynes's novelty was the idea that people would desire to hold fewer cash balances at higher market rates of interest. He called this demand for money relationship the *liquidity preference function*.

Keynes saw the Depression as a collapse of investment

opportunities leading to a low rate of interest. The demand for money would increase as the interest rate fell, causing a drop in total spending. However, Keynes neglected to mention that falling prices created by unemployment would have an effect on expectations of future prices, contributing to a fall in the rate of interest. When aggregate spending fell (in a world of *rigid wages*), the resulting unemployment would destroy new investment opportunities. If the rate of interest fell to extremely low levels, perhaps everyone would hold his wealth in the form of money balances, for the cost of holding them would be so low. If the monetary authorities increased the money supply by purchasing bonds in open market operations, the seller would not use his increased cash to buy other bonds or other assets. He would merely replace his bond holdings with increased money balances. Although the money supply would increase, so would the demand for money. If everyone remained satisfied with these increased money balances, total spending would not increase. In this so-called *liquidity trap* monetary policy could not work.

Few economists take the liquidity trap argument seriously now. What has survived from Keynes's *General Theory*, however, is the general specification of the *liquidity preference function*. Stabilization policy has shifted from the Fed to the President and Congress. Fiscal policy Keynesians believe that the fiscal policy instruments of the Treasury can be used to influence the *demand* for money instead of concentrating stabilization policies in the Federal Reserve's control over the *supply* of money. Specifically, they argue that increased government borrowing (selling more bonds) from the private sector to finance tax reductions or increased government spending will cause market rates of interest to rise. That increase in market interest rates will reduce the demand for money, relative to nominal income, because money will be more expensive to hold. As individuals attempt to reduce their money balances relative to their income by spending more, aggregate demand for goods and services will increase even if the money supply remains constant.

Although the U.S. was not faced with anything like the

Great Depression when Nixon announced to the world his switch to Keynesian economics, monetary restraint had not seemed to be cutting back wage and price inflation very successfully. Nixon certainly had reason to give up on his old friend Dr. Arthur Burns, the man behind the money supply, and join the already swelled ranks of fiscal policy Keynesians.

Economic stabilization policies (monetary and fiscal) have always been hotly debated political issues. Strangely enough, though, one of the most important and powerful bodies determining the level of total spending, the Federal Reserve System, is independent of Congress and the President. The governors of the Fed are each in for 14 years, spanning the terms of several Presidents. The independence enjoyed by the Federal Reserve has touched off occasional bitter criticism of their actions by Presidents Truman, Kennedy, and Johnson. Perhaps no recent President has been so continually victimized by Federal Reserve policy as has Richard Nixon.

The Federal Reserve's power lies in its control of the money supply, which many economists think is one of the principal determinants of total spending. During Nixon's term as Vice President, the recovery from the 1957-58 Recession had barely started to pick up momentum when the Federal Reserve under Chairman William McChesney Martin violently slowed the rate of monetary growth. The money supply had been growing at an annual rate of over 4 percent from the summer of 1958 until the summer of 1959. From the summer of 1959 to the summer of 1960, the money supply actually *fell*.

Richard Nixon's informal economic advisor at the time was Professor Arthur Burns, a pioneer in the research into business cycles. Besides teaching at Columbia, Arthur Burns was the expert on business cycles at the National Bureau of Economic Research in New York. As Chairman of the Council of Economic Advisers in the first Eisenhower administration, Arthur Burns had gone out of his way to instruct Vice President Nixon on economic issues. Burns warned Richard Nixon that the Federal Reserve's actions would result in a recession in 1960. A recession at that point could seriously undermine the Republicans' chances for capturing the Presidency.

Professor Burns's dire forecast proved to be an accurate one. John F. Kennedy was inaugurated President in the midst of the twenty-sixth full-fledged recession in U.S. history. Kennedy had made a campaign promise to get the country moving again. That promise sounded good to a lot of people and the 1960-61 recession cost Nixon the election. Nixon didn't forget the wisdom of Arthur Burns's criticism of Federal Reserve policy in 1959-60.

When President Nixon was elected in 1968, he brought Arthur Burns to Washington as the Special Counselor to the President. At the time that William McChesney Martin's 18-year tenure as Chairman of the Federal Reserve Board ended on January 31, 1970, President Nixon appointed Arthur Burns to replace him. The scholar of business cycles from the National Bureau of Economic Research became chairman of the institution which seemed to have caused so many economic fluctuations. Everyone thought his intimate knowledge of those ups and downs would enable him to keep the economy on an even keel.

But while President Nixon has been dickering with the Congress about the size of the federal deficit, independent Arthur Burns has been turning on and off the money supply level without so much as a hand signal from the administration.

One of the reasons behind the Fed's erratic behavior may be the monetary authority's insisting on looking at interest rates as an indicator of monetary policy, a topic that we shall now examine in detail.

The Fed's Fascination 7
with Interest Rates

During an interview with *Newsweek*, George Meany lamented that Nixon's new economics had not included "... something about interest rates." Representative Wright Patman, Chairman of the House Banking and Currency Committee, has consistently called for federal legislation to fix interest rates. In 1971 he stated on numerous occasions that the so-called prime rate should be fixed low enough "to encourage expansion and production." Representative Al Ullman had told former Treasury Secretary David Kennedy that the only way to halt the recession was to control inflation, lower interest rates, and increase the money supply. When banks started to raise the prime rate in the summer of 1971, Nixon and his advisors spoke out strongly against such increases. But in no other place have interest rates played a key role such as in the Federal Reserve System where they have been viewed as a key policy variable for decades.

There is little doubt that market rates of interest were historically very high prior to Nixon's new game plan. Highest-grade corporate bond yields reached almost 9 percent in 1970 and were still at 7.5 percent in August of 1971. The last time they were anywhere near this level was in 1857.

Historically, interest rates have generally moved with the business cycle, falling in recessions and depressions. Therefore the current situation presents somewhat of an exception to the historical rule. We'll try to explain why in a moment.

When we talk about "the" interest rate we, of course, realize that there is no one single rate. Wright Patman and Richard Nixon seem to like to look at the *prime* rate. This is the interest rate charged very large corporations (which have impeccable financial credentials) for all the money they borrow. The prime rate is usually lower than all other interest rates because there is very little risk of nonrepayment involved. GM is not going to go bankrupt next year.[1] Few expenses are incurred by the banks lending large sums of money to such corporate giants—no credit checks and the like.

The published prime rate can be misleading, though. In recent periods of high inflation, banks have required *compensatory balances* as one requisite for obtaining a loan. Suppose the General Motors Acceptance Corporation wants a $10 million loan from Chase Manhattan Bank. Assume Chase agrees to issue the loan at the published 6 percent prime rate but also requires GMAC to leave $5 million in a non-interest-bearing checking account. The true interest payment is then $600,000 for borrowing effectively only $5 million and GMAC ends up paying 12 percent, not the published 6 percent. Unless one knows what compensatory balances are required for any type of bank loan, one cannot be sure that the reported interest rate is the actual interest charge paid.

There are other long-term interest rates in the economy; we've mentioned the high grade corporate bond interest rate. This is usually referred to as the Aaa (triple A) rate, in reference to the highest grade listing bestowed on corporate bonds by Moody's Investment Service. There are also the municipal bond rates, long-term U.S. government bond rates and the 3- to 5-year government rate.

Shorter-term rates include 90-day U.S. treasury bills, 4-6

---

[1] Rolls-Royce did, though, so big business size does not guarantee eternal financial stability.

month commercial paper, prime bankers' acceptances, and 90-day certificates of deposits.

All interest rates have one thing in common: they represent the price charged by the issuer of the loan for giving to the receiver of the loan command over goods and services today. This "price" varies depending on the length of the loan, the risks involved, and the expected change in the purchasing power of the money involved over the loan's life. The interest rate is not the "price" of money; it is the price of credit.

Interest rates have had a special place in economic theory and this accounts for everyone's concern over them. Since the cost of capital is a large part of the total cost of any businessman's investment, a change in the cost of capital represented by an increase in the interest rate should reduce aggregate investment. Economic theory suggests, then, that rising interest rates would lead to a contraction of economic activity and decreasing rates would have the converse effect. However, historically interest rates have conformed very closely and positively to the business cycle; moreover, the long-term rise in interest rates has accompanied the long-term rise in income.

British economist John Maynard Keynes named this phenomenon Gibson's Paradox after A. H. Gibson, who wrote about it in 1923. Keynes and others attempted to explain the paradox, but an American economist named Irving Fisher had already correctly analyzed the problem back in 1896. Fisher, besides working doggedly for Temperance, pointed out the distinction between the *nominal*, or market, rate of interest and the *real* rate of interest. The nominal rate of interest is the rate at which transactions actually take place. This would be equal to the effective rate of interest that, for example, a businessman has to pay to acquire capital for the expansion of his plant and equipment, taking into account any compensating balances that he has to keep in the lending institution. These market rates of interest measure the rate of exchange, as it were, between dollars today and dollars paid back tomorrow. If the nominal, or market, interest rate is 10 percent, $1 today can be exchanged for $1.10 one year from now. On the other hand, the real rate of interest is sort of an inflation-corrected rate of interest. The real rate of interest is equal to the nominal interest rate minus the expected or anticipated rate of inflation in the future. Individuals make their decisions on how much to save not according to the nominal rate of interest but rather according to the real rate of interest. That is, individuals are interested in knowing what the rate of exchange, as it were, is going to be between goods today and goods tomorrow. Saving decisions are made after taking account of possible inflation eating into the purchasing power of any dollars repaid in the future. The same is true of investment decisions on the part of businessmen. These decisions are a function of the real rate of interest, that is, the nominal rate of interest corrected for any future increases in prices.

Interest rates therefore reflect the interaction of businessmen's anticipations of future sales and profits, the ability of the available technology to produce more goods and services in the future, and individuals' willingness to save. In addition to these factors, the possibility of future inflation decreasing the purchasing power of dollars also enters into any relevant decisions.

Now, if there is no current or expected inflation, the nominal rate is identical to the real rate. The rate of exchange between current and future dollars is the same as the rate of exchange between current and future goods because it takes the same number of dollars to purchase each good in both time periods. Assume that, all of a sudden, prices start increasing at 3 percent a year and this rate of inflation is expected to last indefinitely. If the real rate of interest is, say, 3 percent, the nominal rate of interest must rise to 6 percent because it will take more dollars to purchase each good in the future.

If, on the other hand, inflation is unexpected, it will cause a redistribution of wealth from creditors to debtors because debtors can pay back their debts in dollars of depreciated purchasing power. But if both the creditor and the debtor had anticipated the inflation when their loan agreement was contracted, they would have adjusted things to account for the inflation. The creditor would have demanded a higher interest rate to compensate for the depreciated purchasing power of the dollars he would be repaid. The debtor would have paid those higher rates willingly because he anticipated repayment with depreciated dollars.

One of the authors took out an NDEA loan while in college in the sixties. The interest charge was 3 percent. Since then prices have been rising at 3, 4, 5, and even 6 percent a year. What is the true (purchasing power) cost of a 3 percent loan when prices are rising at 6 percent? The cost is -3 percent, a negative real rate of interest. It's too bad we can't get loans like that today!

The estimated real rate of interest in the U.S. has been amazingly stable, fluctuating very narrowly between 3 and 4 percent. Most changes in nominal rates are due to changes in the expected rate of price change. There was very little inflation from 1960 to 1965; consumer prices rose at only 1.2 percent a year. Beginning in 1965 price rises started to accelerate and continued to rise at ever increasing rates until inflation peaked at over 6 percent annually in early 1970. It appears that people base their expectations of future inflation on recent rates of price changes, for nominal interest rates rose almost in tandem with the rate of inflation. The Corporate Aaa rate was about 4.5 percent in 1965. Since the previous 5 years had averaged only a 1.2 percent rate of price change, it seems likely, then, that the real rate of interest was about 3.5 percent. After 3 years of accelerating inflation the corporate Aaa rate peaked at about 8.5 percent in early 1970. Since prices were rising at a rate of 5.5 percent during 1968 and 1969, the interest rate of 8.5 percent makes the real interest rate seem somewhat low in comparison to 1965.

When the distinction is made between real and nominal interest rates, it is not surprising that periods of inflation are associated with high interest rates, Rep. Wright Patman, Arthur Burns, and Richard Nixon notwithstanding.

Interest rates have had a key role in policy formulations of both the Federal Reserve and the Treasury. The financial press still interprets interest rate changes as an indication of monetary policy changes. For example, in June of 1971, the *Wall Street Journal* remarked that:

> The Federal Reserve System has maintained its restrictive stance in carrying out monetary policy. . . .
> The money managers' restrictive stance was evidenced by a . . . continued upward move in money-market interest rates."

In view of Irving Fisher's 1896 discovery, it is possible that rising nominal interest rates could be viewed as an indication that people expect higher rates of inflation.

Most of the major mistakes made by the Federal Reserve were due to the use of the market interest rate as an indicator of what monetary policy had accomplished. Low or falling market interest rates were interpreted by the Federal Reserve as indicating an expansionary monetary policy, while high or rising interest rates indicated a restrictive monetary policy. The evidence suggests, however, that periods of rapid monetary growth produce inflation. When the inflation is anticipated by the public, the nominal interest rate rises to compensate creditors for the upcoming depreciation in the purchasing power of the dollar. Increases in the rate of monetary growth tend to lower market rates of interest *only* in the short run.

So any higher than normal rate of monetary growth will eventually result in a higher rate of inflation. As the public readjusts their expectations to a higher rate of inflation, the nominal rate of interest will rise until an "inflationary premium" fully compensates creditors for the higher rate of inflation.

At certain times monetary policy was not, however, dictated by interest rate changes. During World War II the Federal Reserve's primary objective was to provide the Treasury with funds adequate to meet all government expenditures. To this end in March 1942 the Open Market Committee asserted its desire to prevent a rise in the interest rates of government bonds during the war. From 1942 until 1951 the Federal Reserve either pegged or supported the rate of interest at a very low level: 2.5 percent on long-term bonds, three-eighths of a percent on 90-day treasury bills. This is one period in which a low interest rate corresponded to expansive monetary policy.

To maintain such a low rate of interest the Federal Reserve had to buy all of the government bonds offered when interest rates started to rise above the support level. Anybody could get cash in exchange for government bonds. Every time the Fed bought a bond, bank reserves increased and there was an expansion of the money supply. The money supply grew 12.1 percent a year from 1939 to 1948 as a result of the Federal Reserve's forced bond purchases. The Federal Reserve had essentially abandoned control over the monetary system during this period of bond support. The Fed felt it was being patriotic.

After the end of the war, the Fed did not at first unpeg the entire interest structure of the federal debt. Only in 1947 did it request such a change in policy. It wanted to unpeg short-term 90-day rates. When the Treasury agreed to this, the Fed finally got some control over liquidity in the economy. But it was not until the Fed-Treasury Accord of March 4, 1951 that full control over the money supply was given back to the Fed.

However, not until 1970 did monetary aggregates, such as the total of currency and demand deposits, become a chief policy decision variable in the eyes of the Fed. At the January meeting of the Open Market Committee, the members stated their desire to have increased emphasis placed on achieving specific rates of growth of certain money aggregates.

Historically, this change was extremely significant. Up to 1970 a typical directive to the account manager of the Open Market Desk of the New York Fed would read:

> . . . to foster financial conditions conducive to resistance of inflationary pressures . . . system open market operations until the

next meeting of the Committee shall be conducted with a view to maintaining firm conditions in the money market. . . .[2]

"Firm" conditions are associated with high interest rates; "easy" conditions mean low interest rates. Obviously numerous policy mistakes are possible using the above logic.

Interest rates have been particularly poor indicators of monetary policy since 1967. After 1967 the rate of inflation accelerated from about 3 percent to over 6 percent. Nominal interest rates therefore rose from 5 percent to over 8 percent. This rise in interest rates fooled the Fed and at the same time gave them an excuse for what was their mistake. During 1968-69 the Open Market Committee issued directives to the Open Market Desk (like the one above) instructing them to maintain "firm" conditions in the money market. What was "firm" to the Fed were the rising market rates of interest. Chairman William McChesney Martin could tell Congress and the President that the Fed was doing its job in the fight against inflation. Meanwhile critics of the Federal Reserve were pointing out that the money supply was increasing at over 7 percent a year, the fastest rate of growth in the money supply in the postwar period.

Surprising as it may seem, the way to produce "firm" money markets (or high market rates of interest) is to increase the rate of monetary growth. This policy may temporarily reduce interest rates. Soon, however, total spending will rise and this will increase the demand for loanable funds. The rate of inflation will accelerate and eventually nominal interest rates will reflect expectations of continued inflation. These "firm" money market conditions are the result of "easy" money.

During the summer of 1971 interest rates and the growth of the money supply were again in the headlines of the financial press. Interest rates rose very rapidly at the same time that the money supply was expanding at phenomenal rates. Incredibly, critics accused the Fed of switching to a restrictive monetary policy because of the rising interest

[2] May 28, 1968 meeting of the FOMC.

rates. On the other hand, those observers watching the growth of the money supply feared that the then current rate of monetary growth was excessive. One can now understand the Nixon administration's confusion concerning monetary policy. By the publication of this book, the Federal Reserve will probably have reverted to the use of interest rates as indicators of monetary policy.

In fact, as far back as May 1971, the Federal Open Market Committee indicated that rapid monetary expansion "would be inconsistent with the orderly reduction in the rate of inflation." In addition, however, the committee was distressed "about the market increase that had occurred in long term interest rates." The very powerful members of that committee, therefore, decided on May 11 that "any firming of money market conditions directed at slowing excessive growth was to be carried out *cautiously*" (emphasis added).

And during a question-and-answer session with the Economic Club of Detroit, Nixon told his audience in September of that same year that whether interest rates remain high or go down "will have a great deal to do with whether we have the Federal Reserve move in."

History does repeat itself.

The Fall of Fixed 8
Exchange Rates

**TREASURY OFFICIAL SAYS "DRAMATIC" STEPS
WON'T SOLVE WORLD'S MONETARY PROBLEMS**

**U.S. HAD DEFICIT IN TRADE IN MAY,
SECOND MONTH IN ROW**

REP. REUSS WOULD LET DOLLAR FLOAT DOWN

The above are headlines from various newspaper articles last year which were concerned with the international monetary crisis. Other countries had been finding themselves with increasing supplies of U.S. dollars. Little more than a decade ago, the headlines said just the reverse; they talked about the dollar shortage problem—the shortage of dollars for world trade and the possibility of trade drying up if international liquidity wasn't increased. To understand the origins of the current international monetary problems, we must go back in history to the *gold standard* which was in effect before the Depression.

Nations operating under the gold standard agreed to redeem their currency in gold when this was requested by any holder of that currency. While gold was not necessarily the means of exchange for world trade, it was the unit to which all currencies under the gold standard were pegged. Since all currencies in the system were linked to gold, exchange rates between those currencies were fixed. Fixing an exchange rate merely means that the price of, say, pounds, is fixed in terms of, say, dollars, and vice versa. Fixing the price of foreign exchange is analytically no different from fixing the price of airplane tickets, of electricity, of natural gas, or of credit. As in all cases with price fixing, there will be market pressures on any price which is not set at a level which equates supply with demand. In order to understand how these problems are ironed out with fixed exchange rates we'll discuss a simple two-nation example.

Assume for the moment that there are no private purchases or sales of financial assets between citizens of different countries. Only goods and services are traded. Let's further assume that the United States and Great Britain are the only two countries which trade with each other. If Americans want to purchase Scotch, they must convert their dollars into pounds. After all, Scotch distillers want to be paid in pounds so that they can pay their workers. On the other hand, British citizens who want to buy IBM typewriters must convert their pounds into dollars. The rate at which pounds can be converted into dollars is called the *exchange rate*. Under the gold standard, exchange rates were fixed because the values of currencies were linked to gold. The price of a pound was, say, $4.00 and the price of a dollar was 5 shillings.

This fixed exchange rate system provided an adjustment mechanism which could eliminate any excess supply or demand for currencies on the foreign exchange market at the fixed exchange rate. Suppose, for example, that pounds are in excess supply on the foreign exchange market at the pegged exchange rate because Britons have purchased more American goods than vice versa. Prices are therefore "too high" in Britain and not "competitive" in the world market. Americans, however, purchase "too few" British goods because of their high price in comparison with American goods.

America is therefore internationally competitive. To prevent a devaluation of the pound—a lowering of its price in terms of American dollars—the British government must be a residual buyer of pounds (seller of foreign currencies or gold). The increased supply of foreign currencies or gold and the increased demand for pounds (brought about by the purchases of pounds by the British government) will eliminate the excess supply of pounds on the foreign exchange market. The exchange rate will remain at its fixed level. However, in the process the total number of pounds in circulation in Britain will have fallen; Britain will have experienced a decrease in her money supply. When an English executive sent away for a new IBM Selectric for his secretary, he sent pounds out of the country. Some were returned when American Scotch lovers bought Scotch with dollars which were then exchanged for pounds. But the rest had to be brought back by the British central bank via its sale of dollars to get those excess pounds. The excess pounds ended up, not in domestic circulation, but in the coffers of the British central bank. Hence the reduction in the British money supply.

Consequently, under the fixed exchange rate rules, any country whose currency was in excess supply automatically experienced a reduction in its money supply. Such a decrease will reduce total spending in that country, lessening the demand for imports as well as the demand for domestic output. As the demand for imported IBM's falls, British citizens will supply fewer pounds to the foreign exchange market. The fall in British prices resulting from the reduction in total spending will induce Americans to purchase more Scotch at the fixed exchange rate, increasing the demand for pounds. Thus, the foreign exchange market will return to equilibrium with the supply and demand for pounds equal at the pegged exchange rate.

If, on the other hand, pounds are in excess *demand* at the pegged exchange rate, the monetary authorities must be residual buyers of foreign currencies or gold and thus suppliers of pounds. Their aim is to prevent the pound from appreciating in terms of the dollar. The process of buying foreign currencies causes the British money supply to expand. The resulting rise in British prices and income will subsequently increase the supply of and reduce the demand for pounds at the fixed exchange rate. The foreign exchange market will again return to equilibrium.

This adjustment mechanism may seem straightforward, but it involves very painful internal business contractions in countries importing more than they are exporting. Internal price adjustments to correct balance of payments deficits are not done overnight.

The essential feature of a truly fixed exchange rate system is that each country's monetary policy can no longer be controlled by the national central bank. The very act of purchasing or selling foreign exchange (currencies) to peg exchange rates produces a change in the money supply which eventually returns the foreign exchange market to equilibrium. No country which submits to a truly fixed exchange rate discipline can have control over its money supply. Rather, it must allow supporting action in the foreign exchange market to determine how much money will domestically be in circulation. The domestic price level must be determined by world prices, therefore.

During the 1930s central banks asserted their independence of this fixed exchange rate discipline. National central banks refused to allow an excess demand or supply of their currency in the foreign exchange markets to affect their own domestic money supplies. They were not going to give *balance of payments* problems priority over domestic economic considerations. For example, if Britain is forced to buy back pounds with its central bank's holdings of dollars, it can replenish its own money supply by buying financial assets (bonds) from private banks. When it buys the bonds, it merely "writes up" the reserves of the bank and thus pounds are put back into circulation because the banks turn around and loan out some of those reserves to Britons who spend that new money.

Any country therefore can insulate its money supply from balance of payments problems by injecting (or withdrawing) money from circulation through buying (or selling) bonds from banks.

These so-called *sterilization policies* will, however, prevent the foreign exchange market from returning to equilibrium. If the money supply remains unaffected, there will be no change in total domestic spending and prices to correct the balance of payments deficit. Excess demand for foreign exchange will persist. Eventually Britain, for example, will run out of foreign exchange (say dollars) to sell in support of its own currency, resulting in a currency "crisis" and eventual devaluation. And that's just what has happened to Britain many times. These currency crises are the outcome of differing monetary policies among nations. If central banks permit their money supplies to adjust in response to foreign exchange stabilization policies, no such crises need occur, but the pain of internal adjustment can be excruciating. Just ask any British subject who has lived through various governmental "austerity" programs. Britons may have wondered why they had to tighten their belts so much just to support the price of pounds.

Truly fixed exchange rates can be maintained only if national monetary policies are coordinated so as to produce the same rate of inflation in all countries whose currencies are pegged to each other. If countries insist on pursuing independent monetary policies, exchange rates must eventually be realigned to reflect differences in purchasing power among currencies. Monetary policies which fail to reflect stabilization operations in the foreign exchange market are the cause of "balance of payments" problems.

In the 1930s practically all countries in the world were in the throes of a devastating and demoralizing depression. Central banks were unwilling to have their money supplies and aggregate demand contract even more just because of a balance of payments deficit. Hence the automatic mechanism by which equilibrium is restored in the foreign exchange market was effectively put in the grave. We could not, therefore, expect a truly fixed exchange rate system to last forever. Virulent economic nationalism, born during the 1930s and surviving today, prevents most countries from allowing their money supplies to be dictated by the actions of people in other countries through the foreign exchange markets. To be sure, some central banks today continue to be residual buyers and sellers of their own currency in times of balance of payments disequilibrium, but through offsetting open market sales and purchases of bonds, they prevent changes in the money supply necessary to restore equilibrium. The mechanism which operated under the gold standard for bringing the foreign exchange market back into equilibrium has been effectively destroyed by sterilization operations.

While the world is no longer on a pure gold standard, fixed exchange rates have remained the rule among most nations until recently. For some time now, though, Canada has had a *floating exchange rate.* Germany, too, has permitted its currency to float for various periods of time. Floating rates permit the foreign exchange rate to return to equilibrium without any effect on the country's money supply. The rate of exchange itself changes instead of the money supply. If countries do not peg exchange rates, supply and demand for currencies on the foreign exchange market will determine the exchange rate.

To illustrate the adjustment mechanism under a floating exchange rate system, let us return to our simplified world consisting of the U.S. and Great Britain. The demand for IBM typewriters by British citizens ends up creating a supply of pounds to the foreign exchange market. On the other hand, the demand for pounds is derived from the demand for Scotch by Americans. Suppose all of a sudden prices in the United States rise by 10 percent while prices in Great Britain remain constant. The exchange rate must change to produce equilibrium in the foreign exchange market in the face of this American inflation.

If exchange rates remain constant, IBM equipment would rise in price relative to British goods in both countries, pricing IBM out of the world market. The American inflation would reduce the supply of pounds to the foreign exchange market at the constant exchange rate because British citizens would buy less IBM equipment at the increased price. The demand for pounds would increase at the fixed exchange rate because Americans would buy more Scotch as the price of IBM equipment increased relative to the price of Scotch.

However, when the exchange rate is allowed to adjust to the changes in supply and demand, the pound will appreciate by 10 percent in terms of the dollar when there is a 10 percent American inflation. In the U.S., American goods will have increased in price by 10 percent, but so will the dollar price of British goods, for it will take 10 percent more dollars to purchase each pound. In Great Britain, the price of British goods will remain constant, but so will the pound price of American goods, for it will take 10 percent fewer pounds to purchase each dollar.

If exchange rates are free to fluctuate in response to private supply and demand, each country can independently pursue its own monetary policy. Some countries may prefer high rates of monetary growth and inflation, while other countries maintain slower rates of monetary growth and price stability. Those countries with higher than average inflation rates will experience a continual devaluation of their currency relative to other currencies. No country's goods will be priced out of the world market through domestic inflation.

In certain South American countries, inflation progresses at rates in excess of 50 to 100 percent per year! The "fixed" exchange rates between Argentina's pesos and U.S. dollars is officially changed several times a year, but never fast enough, because that country and others seem always to have balance of payments problems.

As a contrasting case, Germany has generally maintained a slower rate of monetary expansion and less inflation than have most countries of Western Europe and the United States. The German general wholesale price index was at the same level in 1969 as it was in 1964. During that same time period general wholesale prices in the United States, for example, increased by over 12 percent. As a result of these differing rates of inflation, Germany continued to develop an export surplus. As world prices continued to rise at a faster rate than German prices, German goods became cheaper in comparison with non-German goods. German exports increased rapidly but German imports were discouraged by the rapid increase in world prices at the fixed exchange rate. This trade surplus implies excess demand for Deutschemarks. In order to maintain the fixed exchange rate, the German government has had to purchase foreign exchange (mainly dollars) and sell Deutschemarks on the foreign exchange market.

In November 1969 the German government finally stopped purchasing dollars and other foreign exchange. Immediately the Deutschemark appreciated in value and eventually the German government repegged its value at the new exchange rate. As inflation continued in the United States, the German government again had to purchase large inflows of dollars to prevent the Deutschemark from appreciating. Again in May 1971 the Germans stopped buying dollars and let the mark float up in value in comparison with the dollar. The recent history of the Deutschemark illustrates the difficulties of maintaining fixed exchange rates in the absence of coordinated monetary policies. If countries have different monetary policies resulting in different rates of inflation, exchange rates must eventually be realigned. The rash of currency crises the world has experienced in the last decade are the ultimate consequence of independent monetary policies in a world of fixed exchange rates.

The United States is in a rather special position under the rules of the International Monetary Fund. Under the current international monetary payments system, most countries in the world must peg their currencies to the dollar. Of course, there have been periods where Germany, Canada and other nations have let their currencies float rather than peg their exchange rates to dollars. Other countries have revalued or devalued their currencies in terms of the dollar by changing the exchange rate at which they peg their currency. The United States, though, is under no obligation to peg its currency in terms of other currencies. Until 1968 the United States had to peg the price of gold in terms of the dollar, but since that year even this obligation has been discontinued.

When Secretary of the Treasury Connally told members of the Senate Finance Committee that President Nixon "does not intend to change the price of gold," he apparently didn't understand that it doesn't matter what its price is set at so long as the U.S. continues to refuse to sell any.

Because of the special position of the dollar, it is not meaningful to discuss a "floating" dollar. Whether the dollar changes in value or not in terms of other currencies depends upon the actions of other countries, not the U.S. Since Nixon's speech in August 1971 the U.S. does not even officially peg the price of the dollar in terms of anything. Consequently, many economists refer to the current international monetary system as the "dollar standard."

Floats and Fables 9
of Gold

"I have directed Secretary Connally to suspend temporarily the convertibility of the dollar into gold or other reserve assets, except in amounts and conditions determined to be in the interest of monetary stability and in the best interest of the United States." Two years after the fact, President Nixon announced to the nation and to the world what sophisticated international analysts had already known: the gold standard was laid to rest and the dollar standard officially took its place. International repercussions were to be expected. All Nixon did was hasten the day when other nations realized that they had been lending the United States goods and services in exchange for pieces of paper called dollar bills which bore no interest.

The position of the dollar in the international monetary system has changed radically since the end of World War II. After World War II, free world representatives met in Breton Woods, New Hampshire to create a new international payments system to replace the gold standard. John Maynard Keynes was the head of the British delegation to that Conference. At that time Great Britain was running a huge trade deficit. The pound would have to be devalued unless other countries continued to lend Britain foreign exchange to finance that trade deficit. In addition, Great Britain and the rest of Europe were devastated by the war and needed large amounts of imported capital to rebuild their productive capacity. If these countries had to reduce imports in order to eliminate the trade deficit, recovery from the war would be an agonizingly slow process. In view of Western Europe's situation, it is not surprising that John Maynard Keynes advocated a payments mechanism which would require surplus nations to finance the deficits of other nations by lending them foreign exchange. If surplus nations were forced to lend their foreign exchange to deficit nations indefinitely, fixed exchange rates could be maintained.

The American delegation, headed by Harry Dexter White, fought Keynes's proposal. The United States was a surplus nation which owned most of the world's gold stock. As a trade surplus nation, the United States did not support Keynes's proposal which would have forced the United States to lend foreign exchange to Europe. The American counterproposal was finally adopted and the International Monetary Fund was created. The American plan called for fixed exchange rates and only limited obligations to lend to deficit nations.

Being the good neighbor it was, the United States in the early postwar period voluntarily lent large quantities of dollars to Europe under the Marshall Plan. These loans enabled European countries to finance their imports from the United States. Consequently, the problem Keynes feared concerning Europe's ability to finance the imports needed for recovery was solved by voluntary loans from Uncle Sam.

In the 1960s, however, the tables turned. The United States became a chronic deficit country in her balance of payments, although the balance of trade remained in surplus until 1971. Now the United States favored some arrangement obligating surplus nations like Germany and Japan to lend foreign exchange to deficit nations like the U.S. just as in Keynes's 1945 proposal. To this end, the United States supported the creation of Special Drawing Rights (SDRs) which essentially enabled deficit nations to borrow from surplus nations. Although a modified proposal was adopted by the IMF in 1967, European nations were given a veto on the use of these SDRs. This, in effect, made the loans voluntary rather than an obligation of the surplus countries. Paradoxically, the United States ended up advocating a proposal strongly resembling Keynes's original plan. This time the European nations balked and defeated it. It is understandable that relatively poor Europeans did not feel like lending relatively rich Americans any goods and services they could consume themselves.

Under the IMF rules, the dollar was pegged to gold. The United States was obligated to redeem its currency in gold at $35 an ounce if requested to by a foreign holder of dollars. In effect the United States had to peg the price of gold. The balance of payments deficits of the United States resulted in large gold outflows by the early 1960s. Every Secretary of the Treasury during this period spent part of his tenure in office traveling to Europe to persuade foreign central banks to use their excess dollars to buy American financial securities instead of gold. In other words, we wanted those surplus nations to lend our dollars back. Quite a few countries went along with the American requests, particularly Germany. However, France did not.

De Gaulle continued to demand gold for dollars for two reasons. He thought that any loans given to the United States at that time would enable American companies to buy up industries in France in order to avoid the high tariff wall around the Common Market countries. He feared that French management could not compete with American know-how and that an Americanization of French industry would result. Probably the main reason, though, that he opposed financing the Americans in the balance of payments deficit by lending excess dollars back to the United States was that he felt some of these resources would be devoted to financing the Vietnam war, which he opposed. (He had written Indochina off as a lost cause years before.)

De Gaulle continued purchasing gold from the United States until 1968. In that year the student-worker strike eliminated France's balance of payments surplus. The results of that strike were wage increases and an inflation which put France at a competitive disadvantage in world trade. France no longer had all those excess dollars with which to buy gold. On the contrary! One hot Sunday in August 1969 French President Pompidou was forced to devalue the franc by 14 percent.

Even before the student-worker strike in France, the United States took actions to insulate its gold stock from further losses. In March 1968 the United States took the bold step of announcing that it would no longer sell gold to private holders of dollars. A two-tier system of prices developed. Gold prices were unsupported in the private gold market, but the United States, theoretically, continued to sell gold to foreign central banks at $35 an ounce. However, since 1968, it became quickly evident that the United States would not allow balance of payments problems priority over domestic economic considerations. The United States completely insulated its money supply from outside control by refusing to support the price of gold in the private gold market and by agreeing to sell it to other central banks at $35 per ounce as long as they didn't ask for any. Finally, in his August 15 speech, President Nixon announced that the United States would no longer even pretend to sell gold to foreign central banks at $35 an ounce, thus putting the world officially on a dollar standard. Since United States monetary policy has a tremendous impact on world trade, foreign countries must continue to adjust to the United States's monetary policy.

Consider, for example, the countries whose rate of growth of total spending results in less inflation than the rate produced domestically by the United States's monetary policy. If those countries do not attempt to peg exchange rates, their currencies will appreciate in terms of the dollar. Such has happened in Germany and Japan. The rate of appreciation of their currencies will offset the differences in the rates of inflation.

Alternatively, the central banks in those countries could purchase foreign exchange to prevent their currency from appreciating. As we explained in the previous chapter, if the purchase of foreign exchange is not offset by open market sales of financial securities by the central bank, their money supply will expand, increasing spending. It is in this sense that some European countries accuse the United States of "exporting inflation." The rise in prices and income resulting from the resultant monetary expansion will return the foreign exchange market to equilibrium by equalizing foreign rates of inflation with that of the United States. (So we're still a free world leader.)

Of course other countries' monetary authorities can prevent their respective money supplies from expanding as a result of the purchase of foreign exchange simply by selling bonds in open market operations. But these sterilization operations prevent the foreign exchange market from returning to equilibrium. The central banks would have to continue purchasing foreign exchange to prevent their exchange rates from appreciating. It is important here to note that whenever a country with a balance of payments surplus vis à vis the U.S. decides to sell bonds to its citizens in order to sterilize the impact of foreign exchange operations, that country's citizens are *involuntarily* lending purchasing power to the U.S. Any time a country exports more than it imports, it must somehow lend purchasing power in its own currency to finance the purchase of its goods by foreign countries (unless, of course, foreign countries finance their purchases by drawing down the reserves of foreign exchange). If a country voluntarily lends purchasing power to foreign individuals to finance the export surplus by buying foreign financial securities, there will be no excess supply of foreign exchange at the pegged exchange rate, for the purchase of foreign financial securities constitutes a demand for foreign exchange with which to buy those securities. This voluntary purchase of foreign financial securities enables foreign individuals to bid domestic output away from domestic purchase without creating inflation.

For example, suppose in our two-nation world that Great Britain has a trade surplus with respect to the United States. The United States demands pounds from the foreign exchange market to purchase British goods. Great Britain supplies the foreign exchange market with pounds to purchase American goods. Since Great Britain has a trade surplus (exports exceed imports), the United States will not have sufficient pounds to purchase those British goods unless Great Britain supplies those pounds to the U.S. by purchasing American financial securities. If British citizens voluntarily purchase American financial securities, they reduce their purchasing power available to be spent on goods and services. This reduction in purchasing power is necessary if Great Britain is to sell its output to Americans without equivalent purchases of American output. Americans, on the other hand, have increased purchasing power as a result of the British loan. They can purchase foreign goods without sacrificing an equivalent amount of purchasing power over their own output.

When the British government finances the purchase of foreign exchange (dollars) by selling bonds domestically in open market operations, preventing an expansion of money supply, the private Britons (in the process of buying those government bonds) are indirectly lending purchasing power to the U.S. The purchase of government bonds creates the gap between income and private desired expenditures on goods necessary to finance the export surplus. Private Englishmen are not, however, voluntarily lending purchasing power to finance foreign expenditures on domestic output. If they were willing to voluntarily lend purchasing power to the U.S., there would be no excess supply of foreign exchange. The fact that the government is forced to purchase foreign exchange (or foreign financial securities) and issue its own financial securities to finance the export surplus at the pegged exchange rate is evidence that the private sector would have preferred to use that purchasing power for domestic investment or consumption. Governments eventually will find it unpopular to finance the export surplus by granting loans to deficit countries at rates of return which are unattractive compared to domestic rates. These involuntary loans can be eliminated by allowing domestic inflation or currency revaluation to eliminate any excess supply of foreign exchange.

What are the alternative policy choices facing a country such as Argentina, whose monetary policy produces a higher rate of inflation than that of the United States? If the value of its currency is prevented from depreciating in terms of the dollar, its currency will soon be in excess supply on the foreign exchange market. To peg the exchange rate, the government must sell foreign exchange or gold. This foreign exchange stabilization operation will reduce the money supply, decreasing nominal spending, unless the central bank makes an offsetting purchase of securities in its open market operations. The resulting fall in domestic prices and income will return the foreign exchange market to equilibrium. As we mentioned before, such an internal constriction of an economy can be quite painful.

Any sterilization of foreign exchange operations by open market purchases of financial securities by the central bank prevents the money supply from falling, and the export deficit will persist. The open market purchase of financial securities by the government increases the purchasing power available for private domestic expenditures on goods. Since the money supply remains constant, individuals in the private sector can maintain their money balances and still spend more than their after-tax income only if foreign individuals or the government purchase financial securities from the private sector. Of course the government can peg the exchange rate only as long as it has foreign exchange reserves. Once those foreign exchange reserves are exhausted, the country must devalue its currency. Argentina does it often.

Many countries in the world are having a difficult time adjusting to the dollar standard. The recent inflation in the United States has considerably increased the United States's balance of payments deficit. In fact, for the first time in 20 years, the United States has a continuing trade deficit. Other countries are now deciding they no longer wish to involuntarily lend real resources to the United States. Germany solved the problem by allowing its mark to float in May, 1971. Japan has felt the pressure even more. Japan's export prices have risen only 10 percent since 1963 while U.S. export prices have increased more than 20 percent. Consequently, there was great pressure on the Japanese yen to revalue in terms of the dollar.

The Japanese have relaxed many of their restrictions on imports and the purchase of foreign financial securities in an effort to reduce their balance of payments surplus and also as a result of American threats of import restrictions. For instance, in 1971 they allowed their citizens to invest in the American stock market for the first time. Import quotas on more than 25 products were removed. Japan still had the option of revaluing the yen and that is just what Nixon's import surcharge forced them to do.

Tariffs Bring Joy to 10
the Hearts of Many
(GM, U.S. Steel, and Motorola)

President Nixon's import surtax[1] was a response to the overvaluation of the dollar at the officially pegged exchange rates of several other currencies, especially the Japanese yen. Nixon explained in his August 15 speech that the import surcharge was "an action to make certain that American products will not be at a disadvantage because of unfair exchange rates." In addition, he pledged "when the unfair treatment is ended, the import tax will end as well."

The overvaluation of the dollar has given imports a competitive advantage in several U.S. industries, notably steel, automobiles, and textiles. Remember, though, that imports are financed by the purchase of American exports or by an increase in credit extended the United States by our foreign trading partners. If the United States's money supply is held constant, increased imports have little effect on *total* demand for American goods; they merely shift demand away from import competing goods such as cars and radios to goods produced for export such as computers and goods purchased with that foreign credit (or additional credit supplied by the

[1] See Appendix D for the complete text of the surcharge proclamation.

Federal Reserve to keep the money supply constant). As long as the money supply is not affected, trade deficits need not reduce total effective demand for American goods, although certain industries may feel a real pinch.

Although the overvaluation of the dollar has hurt many U.S. industries, other industries have probably benefited from the resulting trade deficit. Those countries which have a trade surplus with respect to the United States must lend funds to the United States to finance that trade surplus. As a result, many expenditures on American goods can be financed with the foreign credit. For instance, during the first half of 1971 foreigners purchased about $15 billion of U.S. government debt obligations. Had foreigners not contributed so substantially to the supply of loanable funds, the American government would have bid loanable funds away from other sectors of the U.S. economy, such as housing. Consequently, the housing sector probably benefited from the trade deficit, while industries which compete with undervalued imports were hurt.

Since the import surcharge was intended to improve the U.S. position in negotiations aimed at increasing the value of some currencies in terms of the dollar, Nixon must have felt flushed because shortly after his speech the yen was allowed to float up about 6 percent in terms of the dollar. This appreciation of the yen did not, however, reflect a truly free market exchange rate. The Japanese prevented the yen from appreciating further by continuing to purchase large quantities of dollars on the foreign exchange market. The Japanese also imposed additional exchange controls to limit the inflow of dollars. Clearly the Japanese concessions are not satisfactory to the United States, which wants a 10 to 15 percent appreciation of the yen.

As negotiations continue, the original intent of using the import surtax to force a realignment of exchange rates may be obscured as protectionist pressures build on both sides. In the United States some groups are arguing for the use of the import tax as a threat to extract additional concessions from U.S. trading partners. We even heard certain government officials and businessmen express sentiments similar to those Abraham Lincoln once had when he said, "If I buy a Nikon, I have the camera and Japan has my money; but if I buy a Kodak, I have the camera and America has the money."

Certainly American goods face nontariff barriers in many countries. In addition, some government officials advocate using the import surtax to force other free world countries to share the defense burden. There is a danger in asking for too much in exchange for removing the import surtax. Our trading partners may not only refuse to revalue their currencies in terms of the dollar, but may also retaliate by increasing their trade barriers to United States goods.

And that is just what French President Pompidou clearly stated in his news conference on September 23, 1971: M. Pompidou said the Common Market countries must "maintain a common front against the outside world—a united front which will have a great weight the day that a settlement comes." Canadian Prime Minister Pierre Trudeau voiced similar strong objections the same day. He warned that if Nixon's new economic measures became permanent, they would force "fundamental reassessment of U.S.-Canadian relations."

A war of escalating trade barriers on both sides would harm both the United States and our trading partners. Countries trade with each other because they both benefit from that trade. Trade makes it possible for each country to concentrate on producing those products in which it has a comparative advantage. Thus, trade makes it possible for each country to increase the economic value produced with its resources.

The effects of Nixon's temporary tariff increase on the *over-all* welfare of our economy can be shown to harm the economy. Such an analysis does not distinguish between who gains and who loses in the sense that no special weight is attached to the gains of GM as opposed to the losses of stockholders in Sony.

Let's consider the situation where steel is produced in the United States and also imported into the United States. Suppose that the United States can purchase all the steel it wants in the absence of the surcharge at the going world price of steel with the regular tariff added. U.S. producers were not technologically efficient enough to produce all the steel Americans demanded at that price. But, American producers can be induced to furnish more domestically produced steel through an increase in the domestic price of steel. In the face of world competition, this is impossible without raising the tariff.

The imposition of the surcharge means that the domestic price of steel can increase above the previous price of steel, for anyone in the United States who wished to purchase foreign steel must pay the before-tax world price plus the tariff and the surcharge. Now that the effective world price of steel is raised in the domestic economy, U.S. producers of steel can profitably expand their production. They will have to bid resources away from other sectors of the economy, though. The increased production of steel necessitates a reduction of production somewhere else in the economy. Of course, now that domestic production of steel has increased, we will import less. Some resources were used in export producing sectors of the economy to produce the exports needed to exchange for imported steel. Since the imports of steel have been reduced, those resources used in producing exports to exchange for the imports are released to produce other goods. The fact remains, however, that our given stock of resources will yield less steel by reallocating its production to the domestic steel industry. We could have acquired more steel with the same resources if we had left resources in the export producing sector and traded those exports for foreign steel. This is so because of America's *comparative advantage* in the production of the *export* goods.

What about the consumers of steel? When the domestic price of steel rises, less will be demanded by consumers. Manufacturers will use less steel and more substitutes for steel. They have an incentive at the higher domestic price of steel to develop production techniques which minimize the use of steel. As consumers of steel switch to substitutes which are produced domestically, some resources used to produce the exports needed to trade for imported steel will be released from those export industries. These resources can now be used to produce steel substitutes. However the value of these steel substitutes produced will necessarily be less than the value of the imported steel those exports could have been traded for. If not, the resources would already have been used in steel substitute production. The resources were in the export industry to begin with because they had a comparative advantage in the production of exports.

If a war of escalating trade barriers ensues as a result of Nixon's surcharge, *general* economic welfare will be reduced. The United States will get less from the use of its resources because the resources will shift out of, say, export industries and into domestic production of steel or steel substitutes and thus will no longer be used in the areas in which they have a comparative advantage. People will be faced with a set of prices which no longer reflect the social (world) costs of production. Consumers will purchase less steel than is socially optimal and producers in the U.S. will produce more steel than is socially optimal.

The stockholders in U.S. steel will, to be sure, benefit from the Nixon surcharge. So too will workers with talents which are specialized to the steel industry. The same statement can be made for all industries competing with dutiable imports. Nixon's surcharge was specifically aimed at aiding such industries because many of them were experiencing excess capacity in mid-1971. The stockholders and workers in such industries—steel, automobiles, electronics—will no doubt make up a very happy Nixon constituency by November 1972.

What's So New? **11**

A careful analysis of the new economics of Richard Nixon leads to the uneasy feeling that not too much is very new in what he has done since his historic August 1971 speech. However, his interventionist attitude is somewhat of a shock considering the number of about-faces required to arrive at the current level of government economic tinkering.

Nixon found himself in an unpleasant situation in 1971. The inflation he inherited from the Democrats was not slowing down as fast as he thought desirable. Drastic monetary restraint had, however, succeeded in a peaking of inflation by the spring of 1971. The desire on the part of the Fed to get rapidly back to price stability brought with it politically unacceptable levels of unemployment. Nixon and his advisors had no idea that inflationary expectations resulting from 4 years of ever-accelerating inflation would take so long to wane.

With the election little more than a year away, Nixon must have felt he had to act quickly. The wage-price freeze was good window dressing to quell the cries of the Democrats. The tax package proposal was smart thinking because if accepted by Congress it would mean a shifting of demand toward sectors of the economy with excess capacity and unemployment.

The old economics of the Nixon administration was previously concerned with increasing the total level of aggregate demand in order to decrease unemployment. The new economics of Richard Nixon shifted the emphasis in an attempt to direct increased demand into specific sectors of the economy. Eventually such a policy of stabilization of *sectoral* demands, rather than limiting government activity to the stabilization of *total* aggregate demand, will threaten consumer sovereignty.

Structural unemployment may be the symptom of merely a transitional phase needed to affect a transfer of productive resources from one sector to another in response to changes in consumer tastes. For example, if Detroit is experiencing large rates of unemployment because of unfulfilled expectations, that may indicate a shift in consumer taste away from new cars. (It may even be caused by ecology consciousness.) Now, stabilization goals on the part of the Nixon government include the use of excise taxes and tariffs to divert demand away from bottlenecks into industries with excess capacity and deficient demand for labor, such as in Detroit. Consumer preferences will cease to allocate resources if this sectoral demand stabilization is to continue. Resources will be allocated to satisfy government stabilization objectives instead of consumer wants. Consumer tastes will simply tell the government where it has to change other taxes in order to reduce any suffering caused by its policies.

Nixon's desire to stimulate demand in sectors of the economy with excess capacity and high unemployment was not without forethought. These policies were all tied up with his wage and price freeze. The ultimate success of a wage and price freeze depended on the ability of businessmen to hire more workers when demand for their products increased, without having to pay above the prevailing wages. Businessmen in depressed industries certainly had a better chance at hiring additional workers at prevailing wages than did businessmen in industries with no excess capacity and unemployment. So long as rising total aggregate demand could be funnelled into industries with high unemployment rates, wage and price controls would probably not result in shortages. They would then appear "successful." The newest of Nixons would come out as the economic savior of the seventies.

Switching to the international front, Nixon's refusal to convert dollars into gold was merely official recognition that the world had been on a dollar standard anyway since 1968.

The import surtax primarily was put on to benefit such battered industries as steel, automobiles, textiles, and electronics. Nixon apparently never considered the over-all decline in economic welfare that would result. Few people would be mad at the President in November 1972 because the Toyota or Sony they wanted to buy cost more; but quite a few workers and stockholders in those industries just mentioned would still be feeling the flush of a new prosperity.

There is a reason that the study of economics used to be called political economy.

APPENDIX A

Remarks of the President on Nationwide Radio and Television August 15, 1971

Good evening. I have addressed the Nation a number of times over the past two years on the problems of ending a war. Because of the progress we have made toward achieving that goal, this Sunday evening is an appropriate time for us to turn our attention to the challenges of peace.

America today has the best opportunity in this century to achieve two of its greatest ideals: to bring about a full generation of peace and to create a new prosperity without war.

This not only requires bold leadership ready to take bold action—it calls forth the greatness in a great people.

Prosperity without war requires action on three fronts: We must create more and better jobs; we must stop the rise in the cost of living; we must protect the dollar from the attacks of international money speculators.

We are going to take that action—not timidly, not half-heartedly, and not in piecemeal fashion. We are going to move forward to the new prosperity without war as befits a great people—all together, and along a broad front.

The time has come for a new economic policy for the United States. Its targets are unemployment, inflation and international speculation. This is how we are going to attack them.

First, on the subject of jobs. We all know why we have an unemployment problem. Two million workers have been released from the Armed Forces and defense plants because of our success in winding down the war in Vietnam. Putting those people back to work is one of the challenges of peace, and we have begun to make progress. Our unemployment rate today is below the average of the four peacetime years of the 1960s. But we can and must do better than that.

The time has come for American industry, which has produced more jobs at higher real wages than any other industrial system in history to embark on a bold program of new investment in production for peace.

To give that system a powerful new stimulus, I shall ask the Congress, when it reconvenes after its summer recess, to consider as its first priority the enactment of the Job Development Act of 1971.

I will propose to provide the strongest short-term incentive in our history to invest in new machinery and equipment that will create new jobs for Americans: A 10 percent Job Development Credit for one year, effective as of today, with a 5 percent credit after August 15, 1972. This tax credit for investment in new equipment will not only generate new jobs; it will raise productivity and it will make our goods more competitive in the years ahead.

Second, I will propose to repeal the 7 percent excise tax on automobiles, effective today. This will mean a reduction in price of about $200 per car. I shall insist that the American auto industry pass this tax reduction on to the nearly 8 million customers who are buying automobiles this year. Lower prices will mean that more people will be able to afford new cars, and every additional 100,000 cars sold means 25,000 new jobs.

Third, I propose to speed up the personal income tax exemptions scheduled for January 1, 1973 to January 1, 1972—so that taxpayers can deduct an extra $50 for each exemption one year earlier than planned. This increase in consumer spending power will provide a strong boost to the economy in general and to employment in particular.

The tax reductions I am recommending, together with the broad upturn of the economy, which has taken place in the first half of this year, will move us strongly forward toward a goal this nation has not reached since 1956, 15 years ago— prosperity with full employment in peacetime.

Looking to the future, I have directed the Secretary of the Treasury to recommend to the Congress in January new tax proposals for stimulating research and development of new industries and new technologies to help provide the 20 million new jobs that America needs for the young people who will be coming into the job market in the next decade.

To offset the loss of revenue from these tax cuts which directly stimulate new jobs, I have ordered today a $4.7 billion cut in Federal spending.

Tax cuts to stimulate employment must be matched by spending cuts to restrain inflation. To check the rise in the cost of government, I have ordered a postponement of pay raises and a 5 percent cut in government personnel. I have ordered a 10 percent cut in foreign economic aid.

In addition, since the Congress has already delayed action on two of the great initiatives of this Administration, I will ask Congress to amend my proposals to postpone the implementation of Revenue Sharing for three months and Welfare Reform for one year. In this way, I am reordering our budget priorities to concentrate more on achieving full employment.

The second indispensable element of the new prosperity is to stop the rise in the cost of living. One of the cruelest legacies of the artificial prosperity produced by war is inflation. Inflation robs every American. The 20 million who are retired and living on fixed incomes are particularly hard hit. Homemakers find it harder than ever to balance the family budget. And 80 million wage-earners have been on a treadmill. In the four war years between 1965 and 1969 your wage increases were completely eaten up by price increases. Your paychecks were higher, but you were no better off.

We have made progress against the rise in the cost of living. From the high-point of six percent a year in 1969, the rise in consumer prices has been cut to four percent in the first half of 1971. But just as is the case in our fight against unemployment, we can and we must do better than that.

The time has come for decisive action—action that will break the vicious circle of spiraling prices and costs. I am today ordering a freeze on all prices and wages throughout the United States for a period of 90 days. In addition, I call upon corporations to extend the wage-price freeze to all dividends.

I have today appointed a Cost of Living Council within the Government. I have directed this Council to work with leaders of labor and business to set up the proper mechanism for achieving continued price and wage stability after the 90-day freeze is over.

Let me emphasize two characteristics of this action: First, it is temporary. To put the strong, vigorous American economy into a permanent straitjacket would lock in unfairness; it would stifle the expansion of our free enterprise system. And second, while the wage-price freeze will be backed by Government sanctions, if necessary, it will not be accompanied by the establishment of a huge price control bureaucracy. I am relying on the voluntary cooperation of All Americans—each one of you—workers, employers, consumers—to make this freeze work.

Working together, we will break the back of inflation, and we will do it without the mandatory wage and price controls that crush economic and personal freedom.

The third indispensable element in building the new prosperity is closely related to creating new jobs and halting inflation. We must protect the position of the American dollar as a pillar of monetary stability around the world.

In the past seven years, there has been an average of one international monetary crisis every year. Who gains from these crises? Not the workingman; not the investors; and not the real producers of wealth. The gainers are international money speculators. Because they thrive on crises, they help to create them.

In recent weeks, the speculators have been waging an all-out war on the American dollar. The strength of a nation's currency is based on the strength of that nation's economy—and the American economy is by far the strongest in the world. Accordingly, I have directed the Secretary of the Treasury to take the action necessary to defend the dollar against the speculators.

I have directed Secretary Connally to suspend temporarily

the convertibility of the dollar into gold or other reserve assets, except in amounts and conditions determined to be in the interest of monetary stability and in the best interests of the United States.

Now, what is this action, which is very technical? What does it mean for you? Let me lay to rest the bugaboo of what is called devaluation. If you want to buy a foreign car or take a trip abroad, market conditions may cause your dollar to buy slightly less. But if you are among the overwhelming majority of Americans who buy American-made products in America, your dollar will be worth just as much tomorrow as it is today. The effect of this action, in other words, will be to stabilize the dollar. Now, this action will not win us any friends among the international money traders. But our primary concern is with the American workers, and with fair competition around the world.

To our friends abroad, including the many responsible members of the international banking community who are dedicated to stability and the flow of trade, I give this assurance; The United States has always been, and will continue to be, a forward-looking and trustworthy trading partner. In full cooperation with the International Monetary Fund and those who trade with us, we will press for the necessary reforms to set up an urgently needed new international monetary system. Stability and equal treatment is in everybody's best interests. I am determined that the American dollar must never again be a hostage in the hands of the international speculators.

I am taking one further step to protect the dollar, to improve our balance of payments, and to increase sales for Americans. As a temporary measure, I am today imposing an additional tax of 10 percent on goods imported into the United States. This is a better solution for international trade than direct controls on the amount of imports.

This import tax is a temporary action. It isn't directed against any other country. It is an action to make certain that American products will not be at a disadvantage because of unfair exchange rates. When the unfair treatment is ended, the import tax will end as well.

As a result of these actions, the product of American labor will be more competitive, and the unfair edge that some of our foreign competition has had will be removed. That is a major reason why our trade balance has eroded over the past fifteen years.

At the end of World War II the economies of the major industrial nations of Europe and Asia were shattered. To help them get on their feet and to protect their freedom, the United States has provided over the past 25 years $143 billion in foreign aid. This was the right thing for us to do.

Today, largely with our help, they have regained their vitality. They have become our strong competitors, and we welcome their success. But now that other nations are economically strong, the time has come for them to bear their fair share of the burden of defending freedom around the world. The time has come for exchange rates to be set straight and for the major nations to compete as equals. There is no longer any need for the United States to compete with one hand tied behind her back.

The range of actions I have taken, and proposed tonight—on the job front, on the inflation front, on the monetary front—is the most comprehensive New Economic Policy to be undertaken by this nation in four decades.

We are fortunate to live in a nation with an economic system capable of producing for its people the highest standard of living in the world; a system flexible enough to change its ways dramatically when circumstances call for change; and most important—a system resourceful enough to produce prosperity with freedom and opportunity unmatched in the history of nations.

The purposes of the government actions I have announced tonight are to lay the basis for renewed confidence, to make it possible for us to compete fairly with the rest of the world, to open the door to a new prosperity.

But government, with all its powers, does not hold the key to the success of a people. That key, my fellow Americans, is in your hands. A nation, like a person, has to have a certain inner drive in order to succeed. In economic affairs, that inner drive is called the competitive spirit.

Every action I have taken tonight is designed to nurture and stimulate that competitive spirit; to help us snap out of that self-doubt and self-disparagement, that saps our energy and erodes our confidence in ourselves.

Whether this nation stays number one in the world's economy or resigns itself to second, third or fourth place; whether we as a people have faith in ourselves, or lose that faith; whether we hold fast to the strength that makes peace and freedom possible in this world, or lose our grip—all that depends on you, or your competitive spirit, your sense of personal destiny, your pride in your country and in yourself.

We can be certain of this: As the threat of war recedes, the challenge of peaceful competition in the world will greatly increase. We welcome competition, because America is at her greatest when she is called on to compete.

As there always have been in our history, there will be voices urging us to shrink from that challenge of competition, to build a protective wall around ourselves, to crawl into a shell as the rest of the world moves ahead.

Two hundred years ago a man wrote in his diary these words: "Many thinking people believe America has seen its best days." That was written in 1776, just before an American Revolution, at the dawn of the most exciting era in the history of man. Today we hear the echoes of those voices, preaching a gospel of gloom and defeat, saying that same thing: "We have seen our best days." I say, let Americans reply: "Our best days lie ahead."

As we move into a generation of peace, as we blaze the trail toward the new prosperity, I say to every American: Let us raise our spirits. Let us raise our sights. Let all of us contribute all we can to the great and good country that has contributed ever so much to the progress of mankind.

Let us invest in our nation's future; and let us revitalize that faith in ourselves that built a great nation in the past, and will shape the world of the future.

Thank you, and good evening.

APPENDIX B

Economic Stabilization Act of 1970 (as amended) Title II of Public Law 91-379

201. Short title

This title may be cited as the "Economic Stabilization Act of 1970".

202. Presidential authority

a. The President is authorized to issue such orders and regulations as he may deem appropriate to stabilize prices, rents, wages, and salaries at levels not less than those prevailing on May 25, 1970. Such orders and regulations may provide for the making of such adjustments as may be necessary to prevent gross inequities.

b. The authority conferred on the President by this section shall not be exercised with respect to a particular industry or segment of the economy unless the President determines, after taking into account the seasonal nature of employment, the rate of employment or underemployment, and other mitigating factors, that prices or wages in that industry or segment of the economy have increased at a rate which is grossly disproportionate to the rate at which prices or wages have increased in the economy generally.

203. Delegation

The President may delegate the performance of any function under this title to such officers, departments, and agencies of the United States as he may deem appropriate.

204. Penalty

Whoever willfully violates any order or regulation under this title shall be fined not more than $5,000.

205. Injunctions

Whenever it appears to any agency of the United States, authorized by the President to exercise the authority contained in this section to enforce orders and regulations issued under this title, that any person has engaged, is engaged, or is about to engage in any acts or practices constituting a violation of any regulation or order under this title, it may in its discretion bring action, in the proper district court of the United States or the proper United States court of any territory or other place subject to the jurisdiction of the United States, to enjoin such acts or practices, and upon a proper showing a permanent or temporary injunction or restraining order shall be granted without bond. Upon application of the agency, any such court may also issue mandatory injunctions commanding any person to comply with any regulation or order under this title.

206. Expiration

The authority to issue and enforce orders and regulations under this title expires at midnight April 30, 1972, but such expiration shall not affect any proceeding under section 204 for a violation of any such order or regulation, or for the punishment for contempt committed in the violation of any injunction issued under section 205, committed prior to May 1, 1972.

APPENDIX C

Executive Order Providing for Stabilization of Prices, Rents, Wages, and Salaries

Whereas, in order to stabilize the economy, reduce inflation, and minimize unemployment, it is necessary to stabilize prices, rents, wages, and salaries; and

Whereas, the present balance of payments situation makes it especially urgent to stabilize prices, rents, wages, and salaries in order to improve our competitive position in world trade and to protect the purchasing power of the dollar:

Now, therefore, by virtue of the authority vested in me by the Constitution and statutes of the United States, including the Economic Stabilization Act of 1970 (P.L. 91-379, 84 Stat. 799), as amended, it is hereby ordered as follows:

Section 1. (a) Prices, rents, wages, and salaries shall be stabilized for a period of 90 days from the date hereof at levels not greater than the highest of those pertaining to a substantial volume of actual transactions by each individual, business, firm, or other entity of any kind during the 30-day period ending August 14, 1971, for like or similar commodities or services. If no transactions occurred in that period, the ceiling will be the highest price, rent, salary or wage in the nearest preceding 30-day period in which transactions did occur. No person shall charge, assess, or receive, directly or indirectly in any transaction prices or rents in any form higher than those permitted hereunder, and no person shall, directly or indirectly, pay or agree to pay in any transaction wages or salaries in any form, or to use any means to obtain payment of wages and salaries in any form, higher than those permitted hereunder, whether by retroactive increase or otherwise.

(b) Each person engaged in the business of selling or providing commodities or services shall maintain available for public inspection a record of the highest prices or rents charged for such or similar commodities or services during the 30-day period ending August 14, 1971.

(c) The provisions of sections 1 and 2 hereof shall not apply to the prices charged for raw agricultural products.

Section 2. (a) There is hereby established the Cost of Living Council which shall act as an agency of the United States and which is hereinafter referred to as the Council.

(b) The Council shall be composed of the following members: The Secretary of the Treasury, the Secretary of Labor, the Director of the Office of Management and Budget, the Chairman of the Council of Economic Advisers, the Director of the Office of Emergency Preparedness, and the Special Assistant to the President for Consumer Affairs. The Secretary of the Treasury shall serve as Chairman of the Council and the Chairman of the Council of Economic Advisers shall serve as Vice Chairman. The Chairman of the Board of Governors of the Federal Reserve System shall serve as adviser to the Council.

(c) Under the direction of the Chairman of the Council a Special Assistant to the President shall serve as Executive Director of the Council, and the Executive Director is authorized to appoint such personnel as may be necessary to assist the Council in the performance of its functions.

Section 3. (a) Except as otherwise provided herein, there are hereby delegated to the Council all of the powers conferred on the President by the Economic Stabilization Act of 1970.

(b) The Council shall develop and recommend to the President additional policies, mechanisms, and procedures to maintain economic growth without inflationary increases in prices, rents, wages, and salaries after the expiration of the 90-day period specified in Section 1 of this Order.

(c) The Council shall consult with representatives of agriculture, industry, labor and the public concerning the development of policies, mechanisms and procedures to maintain economic growth without inflationary increases in prices, rents, wages, and salaries.

(d) In all of its actions the Council will be guided by the need to maintain consistency of price and wage policies with fiscal, monetary, international and other economic policies of the United States.

(e) The Council shall inform the public, agriculture, industry, and labor concerning the need for controlling inflation and shall encourage and promote voluntary action to that end.

Section 4. (a) The Council, in carrying out the provisions of this Order, may (i) prescribe definitions for any terms used herein, (ii) make exceptions or grant exemptions, (iii) issue regulations and orders, and (iv) take such other actions as it determines to be necessary and appropriate to carry out the purposes of this Order.

(b) The Council may redelegate to any agency, instrumentality or official of the United States any authority under this Order, and may, in administering this Order, utilize the services of any other agencies, Federal or State, as may be available and appropriate.

(c) On request of the Chairman of the Council, each Executive department or agency is authorized and directed, consistent with law, to furnish the Council with available information which the Council may require in the performance of its functions.

(d) All Executive departments and agencies shall furnish such necessary assistance as may be authorized by section 214 of the Act of May 3, 1945, 59 Stat. 134 (31 U.S.C. 691).

Section 5. The Council may require the maintenance of appropriate records or other evidence which are necessary in carrying out the provisions of this Order, and may require any person to maintain and produce for examination such records or other evidence, in such form as it shall require, concerning prices, rents, wages, and salaries and all related matters. The Council may make such exemptions from any requirement otherwise imposed as are consistent with the purpose of this Order. Any type of record or evidence required under regulations issued under this Order shall be retained for such period as the Council may prescribe.

Section 6. The expenses of the Council shall be paid from such funds of the Treasury Department as may be available therefor.

Section 7. (a) Whoever willfully violates this Order or any order or regulation issued under authority of this Order shall be fined not more than $5,000 for each such violation.

(b) The Council shall in its discretion request the Department of Justice to bring actions for injunctions authorized under section 205 of the Economic Stabilization Act of 1970 whenever it appears to the Council that any person has engaged, is engaged, or is about to engage in any acts or practices constituting a violation of any regulation or order issued pursuant to this Order.

THE WHITE HOUSE
August 15, 1971

APPENDIX D

Imposition of Supplemental Duty for Balance of Payments Purposes
4074
By the President of the United States of America
A Proclamation

Whereas, there has been a prolonged decline in the international monetary reserves of the United States, and our trade and international competitive position is seriously threatened and, as a result, our continued ability to assure our security could be impaired;

Whereas, the balance of payments position of the United States requires the imposition of a surcharge on dutiable imports;

Whereas, pursuant to the authority vested in him by the Constitution and the statutes, including, but not limited to, the Tariff Act of 1930, as amended (hereinafter referred to as "the Tariff Act"), and the Trade Expansion Act of 1962 (hereinafter referred to as "the TEA"), the President entered into, and proclaimed tariff rates under, trade agreements with foreign countries;

Whereas, under the Tariff Act, the TEA, and other provisions of law, the President may, at any time, modify or terminate, in whole or in part, any proclamation made under his authority;

Now, therefore, I, Richard Nixon, President of the United States of America, acting under the authority vested in me by the Constitution and the statutes, including, but not limited to, the Tariff Act, and the TEA, respectively, do proclaim as follows:

A. I hereby declare a national emergency during which I call upon the public and private sector to make the efforts necessary to strengthen the international economic position of the United States.

B. (1) I hereby terminate in part for such period as may be necessary and modify prior Presidential Proclamations which carry out trade agreements insofar as such proclamations are inconsistent with, or proclaim duties different from, those made effective pursuant to the terms of this Proclamation.

(2) Such proclamations are suspended only insofar as is required to assess a surcharge in the form of a supplemental duty amounting to 10 percent ad valorem. Such supplemental duty shall be imposed on all dutiable articles imported into the customs territory of the United States from outside thereof, which are entered, or withdrawn from warehouse, for consumption after 12:01 a.m., August 16, 1971, provided, however, that if the imposition of an additional duty of 10 percent ad valorem would cause the total duty or charge payable to exceed the total duty or charge payable at the rate prescribed in column 2 of the Tariff Schedules of the United States, then the column 2 rate shall apply.

C. To implement section B of this Proclamation, the following new subpart shall be inserted after subpart B of part 2 of the Appendix to the Tariff Schedules of the United States:

Subpart C   Temporary Modifications for Balance of Payments Purposes

Subpart C headnotes:
1. This subpart contains modifications of the provisions of the tariff schedules proclaimed by the President in Proclamation 4074.

2. *Additional duties imposed.* The duties provided for in this subpart are cumulative duties which apply in addition to the duties otherwise imposed on the articles involved. The provisions for these duties are effective with respect to articles entered on and after 12:01 a.m., August 16, 1971, and shall continue in effect until modified or terminated by the President or by the Secretary of the Treasury (hereinafter referred to as the Secretary) in accordance with headnote 4 of this subpart.

3. *Limitation on additional duties.* The additional 10 percent rate of duty specified in rate of duty column numbered 1 of item 948.00 shall in no event exceed that rate which, when added to the column numbered 1 rate imposed on the imported article under the appropriate item in schedules 1 through 7 of these schedules, would result in an aggregated rate in excess of the rate provided for such article in rate of duty column numbered 2.

4. For the purposes of this subpart

(a) *Delegation of authority to Secretary.* The Secretary may from time to time take action to reduce, eliminate or reimpose the rate of additional duty herein or to establish exemption therefrom, either generally or with respect to an article which he may specify either generally or as the product of a particular country, if he determines that such action is consistent with safeguarding the balance of payments position of the United States.

(b) *Publication of Secretary's actions.* All actions taken by the Secretary hereunder shall be in the form of modifications of this subpart published in the Federal Register. Any action reimposing the additional duties on an article exempted therefrom by the Secretary shall be effective only with respect to articles entered on and after the date of publication of the action in the Federal Register.

(c) *Authority to prescribe rules and regulations.* The Secretary is authorized to prescribe such rules and regulations as he determines to be necessary or appropriate to carry out the provisions of this subpart.

5. *Articles exempt from the additional duties.* In accordance with determinations made by the Secretary in accordance with headnote 4(a), the following described articles are exempt from the provisions of this subpart:

Item	Article	Rates of Duty	
		1	2
948.00	Articles, except as exempted under headnote 5 of this subpart, which are not free of duty under these schedules and which are the subject of tariff concessions granted by the United States in trade agreements	10% ad val. (see head-note 3 of this subpart)	No change

D. This Proclamation shall be effective 12:01 a.m., August 16, 1971.

In witness whereof, I have hereunto set my hand this fifteenth day of August in the year of our Lord nineteen hundred and seventy-one, and of the Independence of the United States of America the one hundred and ninety-sixth.

RICHARD NIXON

Index

Ackley, Gardner, 14
Agnew, Spiro, 31
Allende, President, 12
Anti-Inflation Act, 1942, 11
Automobiles, 2, 29-30

Black market, 11
Bretton Woods, 54
Brookings Institution, 28
Burns, Arthur, 6 ff, 15, 34-35

Canada, 15
Chile, 12-13
Cigarettes, 11
Comparative advantage, 65
Compensatory balances, 37
Connally, John, 1, 8, 54
Consumer durables, 29

De Gaulle, Charles, 56-57
Depreciation, 25-26
Depression, Great, 31
Dividends, 24
Dollar standard, 53 ff

Economic Report of the President, 13
Economic Stabilization Act, 2, 77-78
Evans, Michael K., 28
Expectations, 15

Federal Reserve, 3 ff, 27, 32 ff, 41
Fiscal policy, 2, 25 ff, 31 ff
Fisher, Irving, 38
Fixed exchange rates, 46 ff
Floating exchange rate, 50 ff
Friedman, Milton, 31

Galbraith, John K., 8*n.*, 10, 17 ff
Germany, 11 ff
Gibson's Paradox, 38
Gold standard, 45 ff
Guidelines, 13 ff

Hodgson, James B., 3
Holland, 14
Hyperinflation, 12

Inflation:
    expected, 39
    unexpected, 39
Interest rates, 33 ff
International Monetary Fund, 52
Investment tax credit, 2, 25 ff

Job Development Credit (*see* Investment tax credit)
Johnson, L. B., 2, 5

Kennedy, David, 36
Kennedy, John, 4, 25
Keynes, John M., 31 ff, 38, 54-55

Labor productivity, 22
Liquidity preference function, 32-33
Liquidity trap, 33

McCracken, Paul, 8, 17, 20
Martin, William McChesney, 4, 5, 34, 43
Marshall Plan, 55
Meany, George, 2, 23, 36
Money supply, 4, 6, 32, 34
Moody's Investment Service, 37

National Bureau of Economic Research, 34
Nominal rate of interest, 38

Office of Economic Stabilization, 11
Office of Price Administration, 10
Office of War Mobilization, 11

Open Market Committee, 41 ff
Open Market Desk, 42

Patman, Wright, 36-37
Perry, George, 28
Playboy, 10
Pompidou, Georges, 57, 64
Price Control Act, 1942, 8
Prime rate, 37
Profits, 23-24

Real rate of interest, 38
Real wages, 16
Recession, inflationary, 4
Reserves, bank, 4

Sheahan, John, 14
Shultz, George, 8
Special Drawing Rights (SDRs), 56
Stabilization policies, 33 ff
Sterilization policies, 49
Structural unemployment, 68
Supply of labor, 22
Surcharge, import, 2, 62 ff, 83-86

Tariffs, 62 ff
Taxes, 27
Treaty of Versailles, 11
Trudeau, Pierre, 64

Ullman, Al, 3
Unions, 9

Vietnam, 5, 56

Wage and price freeze, 1, 2, 9, 17 ff, 79-82
Washington Post, 17n.
White, Harry Dexter, 55